WAGON

The Television Series

TRAIN

By James Rosin

James Rosin (signature)

Published by THE AUTUMN ROAD COMPANY, Philadelphia, PA

Library of Congress Control Number
2008901942

ISBN 13: 978-0-9728684-4-0
ISBN 10: 0-9728684-4-5

Design by Ron Dorfman, Warminster, PA

*Printed by Wentworth, A Consolidated Graphics Company
Columbia, SC*

Also by JAMES ROSIN:

PHILLY HOOPS: The SPHAS and Warriors

ROCK, RHYTHM AND BLUES

PHILADELPHIA: City of Music

ROUTE 66: The Television Series 1960–1964

NAKED CITY: The Television Series

CONTENTS

FOREWORD

STORYTELLERS have been important to all societies. Their responsibility was to pass on the culture, the way of life to the next generation. Gathering around the campfire or in front of the fireplace with our grandparents, parents, friends and neighbors, our children learned through storytelling what worked and didn't work in life. We learned how to survive, set goals, find happiness, make friends, have lifelong relationships and achieve our dreams. We learned how to handle setbacks and develop the tools necessary to succeed. Life is good! Life is a team sport!

More people watch an episode of prime time television in one hour than see a Broadway play in ten years, or read a best-selling book in twenty years, or listen to a story told around a campfire in a lifetime.

Each *Wagon Train* show had twenty to thirty million people sitting around their "electric bonfires"—television sets. They'd bring their family and friends in to listen and watch a story without interruption from storms, stampedes or hostile folks. That is what television means to storytellers. It gives them the opportunity to tell entertaining and fascinating stories to an unbelievably large audience.

Wagon Train was a Conestoga classroom—a prairie schooler—about our country's westward expansion, about people looking for a new life, a fresh start. It was also an anthology—a collection of short stories that were morality plays about rugged people that lived these stories.

Television and re-runs enable us to relive the adventures of pioneers, mountain men, wagonmasters and scouts back when our country was young, when the frontier was out west and not outer space. Jim Rosin researched *Wagon Train's* successful eight-year run on television. He interviewed actors, writers, producers, directors and others that helped tell two hundred and eighty four stories. We can read the stories behind the stories. Many photographs of the players are worth thousands of memories! Hopefully you'll take prime time to read about the history of *Wagon Train*—one of television's most popular western series.

— DENNY MILLER
(Duke Shannon 1961–1964)

ACKNOWLEDGEMENTS

I WOULD like to thank the following people who generously took time to contribute to the content of this book: Robert Horton, Denny Miller, Robert Fuller, Ernest Borgnine, James Drury, Dana Wynter, Harry Carey, Jr., Debra Paget, L. Q. Jones, Morgan Woodward, Peter Brown, William Smith, Gregory Walcott, Diane Foster, Greg Palmer, Joseph Pevney, Warren Stevens, Beverly Washburn, James Lydon, Tommy Sands, James H. Brown, Boyd Magers, Gary Yoggy, Paul Savage, Harry Flynn, Frederick Shorr, John Christie, Francis Nevins, Alicia Williams, and the website: RobertHorton.com.

PREFACE

FORTUNATELY, I came along at the right place and time for a full appreciation of all westerns—the late '40s-early '60s.

I grew up with a western influence in Independence, Kansas (near where the Dalton and James gangs rode) and Ponca City, Oklahoma (the site of the famed 101 Ranch). Beginning in late 1946 at the Beldorf Theater in Independence and the Center in Ponca City, you could ride the range with the current crop of B-western heroes—Gene Autry, Monte Hale, Tim Holt, Eddie Dean, Jimmy Wakely, Roy Rogers, Charles Starrett, Johnny Mack Brown, and others. By 1953 the new medium of television offered a steady hour upon hour appreciation of the early screen cowboys—Buck Jones, Bob Steele, Hoot Gibson, Ken Maynard, George O'Brien, Rex Bell, Tim McCoy and the rest. The early '50s was also the time for the dawning of the TV western—Gene Autry, Roy Rogers, Annie Oakley, Hopalong Cassidy, Wild Bill Hickock, Kit Carson, Cisco Kid and others which slowly matured into the so-called adult TV western from the late '50s to the early '60s: *Gunsmoke, Cheyenne, Have Gun Will Travel, The Rifleman, Rawhide, Sugarfoot, Bronco* and dozens more, including the acclaimed *Wagon Train.* Much of the appeal of *Wagon Train* was the camaraderie of the wagonmaster, his scouts, cook and assistant wagonmaster who all had a common goal—they were dedicated to seeing that everyone on the wagon train arrived safely in California. Although the cast of *Wagon Train* evolved and changed during its eight year journey, each member of the cast—Ward Bond, Robert Horton, Terry Wilson, Frank McGrath, Denny Miller, John McIntire, Michael Burns, Robert Fuller—brought a unique and different personality to the show. It became a television series that many people remember with appreciation and fondness.

— BOYD MAGERS
Author and Western Historian

THE WAGON TRAIN JOURNEY

IN the mid-1800s, large numbers of people began to migrate from the Midwest to the promised land of California and Oregon. Travelers were willing to make the 2000 mile journey across difficult terrain. They sought to escape the harsh weather and fever-infested swamps of the Midwest to live in the sunshine and on the fertile land of the western frontier.

When Congress passed the Homesteads Act, it gave the head of a family the right to acquire 160 acres of land, settle on it, cultivate it for five years, and then be granted ownership. It was estimated that throughout the 1840s, over 14,000 people migrated west. The number of travelers increased dramatically with the passing of the Homesteads Act in 1862. By 1890, all available federal land had been settled by these pioneers.

The trip cost a man and his family about $1,000. They traveled in a specially prepared wagon that cost about $400. The wagon and the wheels were mainly made of wood with iron sparingly used at crucial points to reinforce the overall structure. The canvas top was waterproofed with linseed oil and stretched over a framework of hoop-shaped slats. The wagons were packed with food supplies, including flour, bacon, beans, fruit, coffee, salt and lard; cooking utensils and water kegs.

There was little room in the wagon for people except for children and the elderly. The remainder of the family walked beside the wagon or rode on horseback.

Oxen, mules and horses were used to pull the wagons. Oxen were the most popular. They were cheaper, stronger, and easier to work with than horses. They were also less likely to be stolen by Native Americans on the trip west, and would be more useful as a farm animal once the settler reached his destination.

The chief causes of death on the journey were accidental shootings, drownings, and disease.

The wagon train traveled about two miles an hour and about ten miles a day. With good weather, the 2000 mile journey from St. Joseph and Independence, Missouri to California and Oregon took about five months.

WAGON TRAIN:
About the Series

WAGON TRAIN debuted on Wednesday night, September 18, 1957 from 7:30 P.M. to 8:30 P.M. on the NBC Television Network.

The television series was initially inspired by the 1950 John Ford film, *Wagonmaster*. The movie concerned a group of Mormons led by Elder Wiggs (portrayed by Ward Bond) as they traveled through 1840s Utah territory in search of a new home. They were guided by two horse traders: Travis Blue (Ben Johnson) and Sandy (Harry Carey, Jr.), who functioned as wagonmaster and guide respectively. Johnson and Carey were perfectly cast. They were two of the finest horseback riders in the film industry.

HARRY CAREY, JR.
(Wagonmaster Co-Star)

We were both very comfortable on horses. Ben (Johnson) was a professional cowboy and I had been around horses since I was four years old. Ford understood the habits of horses and knew how unpredictable they could be. He would shoot his close angle dialogue scenes with actors on horses first, then do his run-by shots or action sequences. If you did it in reverse, the horses would be restless and move around. If you got in tight on them, they'd move out of frame, then you'd have to shoot the scene again. It was hard enough to get them to do the same thing again and again, so this way helped a great deal. Besides, it was not Ford's nature to do take after take with horses or humans. He usually shot a scene once, got it right, and that was it. He was able to accomplish that because he never over-rehearsed an actor. He felt they'd lose their energy and spontaneity. He knew what he was doing. He had four Academy Awards and probably should have had ten.[1]

Seven years later, with night-time television westerns gaining popularity, Revue Studios developed *Wagon Train* as an hour-long weekly television series. Revue was a division of MCA (Musical Corporation of America) that produced late 1950s television series such as *Alfred Hitchcock Presents, Leave It to Beaver, Tales of Wells Fargo, Restless Gun, Cimarron City, Mike Hammer, Riverboat* and *Laramie*.

Ward Bond was cast as Wagonmaster Major Seth Adams, a retired U.S. Army Officer who guided the wagon train on the journey west from St. Joseph, MO to Sacramento, CA. Bond had enjoyed a prolific career as a supporting actor in feature films. Along the way he appeared in such memorable movies as *It Happened One Night, Gone With the Wind, The Grapes of Wrath, The Maltese Falcon, Gentleman Jim, It's a Wonderful Life, The Quiet Man, The Searchers* and numerous others. Bond was a colorful, larger-than-life performer. He was a perfect choice for the role of Seth Adams, a burly, temperamental, no-nonsense authority figure who was also a concerned and caring individual despite his sometimes gruff nature.

GARY YOGGY
(Author)

The humanity and compassion of Seth Adams was demonstrated from the very first episode in *The Willy Moran Story*. Adams rescues an old friend with whom he had served at Gettysburg during the Civil War from a street brawl, and gives him a job on the wagon train, despite his obvious addiction to alcohol. Adam's faith later proves justified when Willy risks his life to save the train from an assault by Quantrell's Raiders. Throughout the first three-and-a-half seasons, Adams is continually helping those in need, including a young man who has lost his horse (*The Rutledge Monroe Story*—5/21/58), a youth in shock after seeing his father lynched (*The Juan Ortega Story*—10/8/58), a man who's been beaten and left on the trail for dead (*The Joshua Gilliam Story*—3/30/60), and a fatherless crippled boy (*The Dick Jarvis Story*—5/18/60).[2]

Robert Horton was cast in the other lead role as Flint McCullough, the young, brash and self-assured wagon train scout. Horton had worked in films and television from the early 1950s. Horton too was a very appropriate choice for the role. He was handsome, lean, and exuded much of the charm and self-confidence inherent in his character.

ROBERT HORTON
(Flint McCullough 1957–1962)

Once I was cast in the role, I wrote a biographical sketch of Flint McCullough so that the writers would not have a different point of view about me every time they wrote a script. Eventually, that was embraced by the writers; so I was able to fashion the character out of what I wrote.

"Flint was born in 1839 in Virginia, the son of a middle class family. His mother was a native of Virginia, his father an immigrant from Scotland who earned his living as a teacher at Virginia's College of William and Mary.

"By selecting the teaching profession as his father's occupation, and by choosing Virginia as his mother's home, I feel that both a certain grace in his everyday living habits can (easily) be explained, as the old South was certainly the home of graciousness in early America, and also his early contact with education would not be too difficult to understand.

"In 1850 his family moved from Virginia and headed west for Salt Lake City. I chose this year, as this was the year the University of Utah was founded. This would give a logical reason for the move from the father's standpoint economically, and if you chose to have him interested in or converted to the Mormon faith, you would only double the motivation. This would also give young "Flint," now eleven, his first contact with the problems of crossing the plains, acquaint him with the Oregon Trail as far as the South Pass, and then through the pass to Fort Bridger, and on to Salt Lake. As you know, this route was the route of the Donner Party, the Mormons, and a great majority of those pushing on to California.

"In the winter of 1852 the Mormons had a particularly bad cold season, and during this winter, in my story, I chose to have Flint's father pass away with pneumonia. This I felt would aid in Flint's maturation, as now he, in essence, would be the head of the family. This would also serve in motivating an even closer relationship between him and Jim Bridger, the latter becoming a kind of father. This relationship now opens up and explains Flint's understanding of Indians. The Mormon people were on friendly terms with the Ute tribe, and this tribe spoke a dialect of the Siouan language, one of the great linguistic families of the North American Indians, engulfing nearly all the tribes who lived between the Mississippi River and the Rocky Mountains. Add to this the fact that Bridger had two wives, both squaws, picturesquely named, Blast Your Hide, a Cheyenne, and Dang Your Eyes, an Arapahoe, and you further explain Flint's understanding and acceptance of Indians and their customs, and as he was Jim Bridger's friend, the Indians accepted him. Bridger was celebrated across the frontier as a scout, trapper, hunter, and fur trader, and by linking Flint's life with his, from 1850 through 1857, the how in my characterization of Flint can be gradually explained.

"To continue, in 1855 Bridger returned East, and ultimately was hired as a scout by General Albert Sydney Johnston. In my story Flint goes with him, crosses the plains for the second time, and with the advent of the Civil War why shouldn't Flint cast his lot with the South. After all, his mother was from Virginia.

"At the end of the Civil War, with the South in ruin, Flint returns to the thing he knows best: the frontier. The last I heard of him, he was scouting for Major Adam's wagon train traveling from St. Joseph, MO to Sacramento, CA."[3]

The relationship between wagonmaster Adams and his frontier scout could be intense and turbulent as well as humorous and light-hearted.

ROBERT HORTON

When I first met Ward, I had nothing but admiration and respect for him. I had watched him in many films over the years. I thought his performance in *Gentleman Jim* as John L. Sullivan was as good as it gets. However, very early on, I became aware that we really didn't have very much in common. We honestly didn't relate at all. At the same time, we enjoyed a great rapport on camera.[3]

BOYD MAGERS
(Editor and Publisher: Western Clippings*)*
I think what made *Wagon Train* work was Robert Horton's relationship with Ward Bond. They were polar opposites in background, politics, and life, as well as on the show. I believe that underlying current of two very contrasting individuals gave the show a spark.[4]

ROBERT HORTON
I enjoyed working with Ward. He was always right there. He looked you in the eye and said his lines with honesty and conviction. In all of our scenes, whether they were of agreement, disagreement, humor or whatever took place in the moment, Ward and I worked marvelously together. In fact, I think the relationship between Major Adams and Flint McCullough on screen was as good as Gable and Tracy. It was perfect. He'd be hollering at me at every possible moment, and I'd be smiling back as I rode away from him.[3]

The chemistry between Bond and Horton solidified the show and drew millions of viewers in the process. *Wagon Train* ranked number 23 in the Nielsen ratings during its first season (1957–1958), rose to number 2 for seasons two through four (1958–1961) becoming the top-rated show in its fifth season (1961–1962). Two other regular cast members that contributed to the show's stability were ramrod and assistant wagonmaster Bill Hawks (Terry Wilson) and chief cook and bottle washer Charlie Wooster (Frank McGrath) whose recipes and opinions were a constant source of frustration to the Major. Both Wilson and McGrath were well-seasoned stuntmen and long-time friends and associates of Ward Bond. They had all worked together on numerous John Ford films. When Bond signed to do *Wagon Train*, he insisted that both of them join the show. Gradually during the first season, their roles grew larger and they were given more things to do. Eventually, they became an integral part of the series.

L. Q. JONES
(Multiple Appearances)

Frank was a great stuntman and he was tough. One time they thought he had a heart attack, so they called an ambulance to take him to the hospital. No one was sure he would make it. Well, once the ambulance left the studio, Frank made 'em stop at the liquor store across the street so he could pick up a "fifth." Now that's tough!

Frank had been "doubling" and doing stunts sine the late 1930s; but he had his own way of doing things, and he didn't believe in using some of the safety devices they developed over the years.

About a year before *Wagon Train* began, I was doing a picture at Warner Bros called Santiago (with Alan Ladd). Frank was doubling a Spaniard who gets shot off his horse, gets caught in the stirrup, and gets dragged a bit before he falls away. Most stuntmen would install a "dead man" (a releasing device where you trip a lever or pull a rope which releases your foot) to get you out of the stunt before it becomes dangerous. Not Frank. So they shoot the scene, Frank falls off, and now he can't get his foot out of the stirrup. The horse is draggin' him across this narrow foot bridge, and Frank is bangin' his head against the posts of the bridge. To make matters worse, Frank is bumpin' into the horse's hoofs which spooks the horse. We finally catch up to him down the road and Frank is bruised and bloodied. But Frank was tough and kept on. He took a lickin' and kept on tickin'![5]

HARRY CAREY, JR.
(Multiple Appearances)

Wagon Train was a different kind of western and not your routine "shoot-em-up." Ward had a lot to do with the show's success. He was a strong, powerful actor who had showcased himself in many John Ford films, and he was fresh off a colorful portrayal as Samuel Clayton in *The Searchers* which was probably one of the best westerns ever made. Ward also had a great personality for television and he was marvelous as the wagonmaster.[1]

GREG PALMER
(Multiple Appearances)

Ward was a man's man. He had a great presence on screen and a lot of strength. When you worked with him, he gave you a lot to work off of, which kept you on track.[6]

GREGORY WALCOTT
(Multiple Appearances)

One thing I noticed about Ward Bond was that he responded to strength in turn. So in my scenes with him, I would strive to be as strong and purposeful as I could when called for, and he responded to that. We did some good work together and got along very well.[7]

BEVERLY WASHBURN
(Multiple Appearances)

I was in one of the first episodes filmed in the summer of 1957. I was about 13 or 14 years old at the time. Ward Bond was a nice man who would also use some colorful language. Because I was a minor, they had what was called a "welfare worker" on the set. She was a teacher from the Los Angeles Board of Education that was there to look out for my interests. At one point, she went to the producer and said if he used one more swear word, she would pull me from the set. So the producer spoke to Ward Bond. Later he came over to me and apologized. I don't think he was used to having a child actor on the set. He was used to being around a lot of men; but from then on, he was very aware of my presence and I never heard another swear word. He was really a kind-hearted man, always very nice to me. I did two more episodes with him. In fact, to this day, I have a picture of him on the wall in my house, that he autographed. It says, *"To Beverly, the finest little actress. Ward Bond."*[8]

GARY YOGGY

Bond put much of himself into the character, took great interest in the show and had considerable influence over its production. He once rejected a script in which a woman was murdered for no apparent reason. Bond felt the killer would be portrayed as a psychopath and flatly stated that "Nobody is going to make me play in a story with a degenerate in it on a TV show children are watching." Production was held up for two days on another occasion while Bond and the show's staff rewrote sixty-three pages of a seventy-page script that he found offensive.[2]

Wagon Train was the first western anthology series on network television that became popular right from the start. In 1959 when it was attracting millions of British viewers as well, the Labour party raised the issue that the General Election in Britain should not be held on the same day *Wagon Train* was shown because it would keep so many labour supporters out of the polling booths.

GREG PALMER

Wagon Train appealed to a lot of people because it exposed the open wilderness and countryside of an earlier time. It gave us an idea of what it was like for people traveling across the frontier and as they passed through hostile terrain and endured hardship. It was very appealing to watch the adventures and drama of people living in an early western era.[6]

GARY YOGGY

In *The Horace Best Story* (10/5/60), Major Adams has a meaningful message about the awesome burdens and responsibilities of being a wagonmaster. When his cousin Horace, who too wants to be a wagonmaster, says he will do his best, Major Adams replies:

"That's all any man can ask of you. But you know so many times the best is just not good enough… when you think of all the people—seventy-five or a hundred of 'em who are gonna die when the cholera hits your camp without you knowin' it's comin'… and that Indian war party that comes down off the high hills. Their screams splinter the night and their arrows set fire to it… you say, well, I did my best. That's what you say to all those silent dead. I did my best… you know your heart begins to falter a bit and you begin to wonder with all those people lookin' to ya, dependin' on your judgment, willin' to follow you into the wilderness. Then you come to the mountains. Of course, the mountains are usually covered with rock and shale and the wagon wheels slip and slide back and they break and then yer wagon itself lurches backwards and the horse collars cut into the bleeding shoulders of yer horses. Yes sir, those barren hillsides when ya knew there was gonna be grass, but there wasn't any grass and then ya come on a dry creek bed where you was sure there was gonna be water, but there isn't any water. Yer people are thirsty. All those moments of decision Horace, those are the tough moments. You have to decide whether to cross the river at night or whether yer gonna wait til dawn… whether ya want to take the uncharted short cut or the long mountain trail that's safe… and all the time you feel that those people are lookin' at ya and waitin'. They're yer people Horace, yer people…so finally ya have to make a decision to move on and at that minute, Horace, you pray that Almighty God is close to your hand when you make that decision…"[2]

Another significant part of the show were the travelers on the wagon train. Many of the storylines revolved around their trials and tribulations as they journeyed west to California. The anthology format provided the opportunity for a wide variety of stories highlighting richly-drawn dimensional characters in well-written teleplays. This attracted many top-notch actors from the movie and television genre. In the first two seasons alone, the guest stars included: Ernest Borgnine, Ricardo Montalban, Michael Rennie, Sterling Hayden, Shelley Winters, Mercedes McCambridge, Eddie Albert, Farley Granger, Agnes Moorehead, Guy Madison, Nina Foch, Shepperd Strudwick, Dan Duryea, Robert Sterling, Anne Jeffreys, Keenan Wynn, George Montgomery, James Whitmore, Linda Darnell, John Carradine, Gilbert Roland, Debra Paget, Charles Bickford, Forrest Tucker, James Dunn, Marjorie Main, Reed Hadley, Lee Van Cleef, Lou Costello, Bette Davis, Jane Wyman, Rhonda Fleming, Cliff Robertson, Virginia Mayo, Brian Donlevy, Jan Sterling, Andy Clyde, and Vera Miles.

DEBRA PAGET
(Guest Star: The Marie Dupree Story *and* The Stagecoach Story*)*
I was under contract to 20th Century Fox for ten years and

I had mainly worked in features before I did my first *Wagon Train (The Marie Dupree Story)*. But I began to do television to broaden my opportunities. I was fourteen when I was placed under contract to 20th, so when you've been somewhere and grown up there like I had, they come to have a certain concept of who and what you are. Doing television provided something extra that added a lot more variety and *Wagon Train* was so well done. They had wonderful stories about people, and Bob Horton and Ward Bond were very gracious. I did two episodes and they were both very nice experiences for me.[9]

BEVERLY WASHBURN

When I was cast in my second *Wagon Train* I found out I'd be working with Lou Costello. I was a huge Abbott and Costello fan so I couldn't wait to work with him. Lou Costello was hilarious because he could never remember his dialog. He was used to ad-libbing in a lot of his comic routines and it had been a while since he had to stick to a script. Every time he'd go up on his lines, instead of apologizing, he's look straight in the camera and say, "So how are you, Ward?" He was a wonderful man and very kind to me. I believe that was the only dramatic role he ever did. The show was written by Harry Von Zell (from *The Burns and Allen Show*) who also played the heavy. Shortly after Lou worked with me, he wrote a little book with the help of his daughter, Chris, and in it was a little paragraph about me. He mentioned the *Wagon Train* episode we did and said, "There was this little girl in it and I couldn't have done it without her. Her name is Beverly Washburn." I was very touched. Not long after that he passed away.[8]

JAMES BROWN
(First Assistant Director 1958–1961)

I remember working with Bette Davis who did several guest appearances. Aside from having one of the greatest screen presences ever, she was a total professional. She was aware of everything on the set that pertained to her when she was in front of the camera. She could tell the script supervisor on what line she moved her hand to reach for the coffee cup when they were matching shots. She never had to be told when to do anything.[10]

DENNY "SCOTT" MILLER
(Duke Shannon 1961–1964)

I remember working with Bette Davis on the show. We were about to do a rehearsal, so Ms. Davis and I took our places facing each other next to a Conestoga Wagon. The director called "Action." I said my line and she stared back at me with those Bette Davis eyes. It felt like the longest moment of my life. But it wasn't. The next one was. She turned away without saying her line, walked over to the director and said loud enough for everyone to hear, "Is he going to say it that way?" The director was almost as stunned as I was. He explained to her that was my character, a shy cowboy who was more comfortable talking to his horse than to a woman. She whirled around, strode back to her mark and barked, "Give it to me again." This time I said my line and she responded. I don't remember how the rest of the scene went, but when it was over, I was as relieved as someone leaving the dentist's chair after a root canal.

The next day I saw something I had never seen before. In all the years I had known John McIntire, I had never seen him angry. He was a very kind and easy-going man. Not that day. He was pacing back and forth with his fist clenched and breathing hard. We didn't know what had made him so mad, but we knew who had—Ms. Davis had struck again![11]

Academy Award-winning actor Ernst Borgnine was another actor who guest- starred in multiple episodes. He appeared in a total of five.

ROBERT HORTON

When we filmed *The Willie Moran Story* with Ernie, it was not supposed to be the lead-off show of the series. (*The Jean LeBec Story* was.) However, he was so good in it, his character and the story so appealing, that NBC decided it would be the premier episode of *Wagon Train* in the fall of 1957. Ernie was one of the strongest actors I ever worked with, and one of the nicest. I did a show with him in the fourth season (*The Earl Packer Story*) that remains one of my favorites.[3]

ERNEST BORGNINE
(Guest Star: Multiple Episodes)

In the Spring of 1965, I was working on *McHale's Navy* on the Universal lot when someone told me they were doing the final episode of *Wagon Train.* I said, "What? I was in the first one aired. I gotta be in the last one filmed." So I took time out, I went up to the producer's office and said "Howard (Christie), you rascal, what are you doin'? You're makin' the last one without me?" Howard said, "Ernie, the only thing left is a bit part of an elderly Indian." "I'll play 'im," I said. So I put on the wig and outfit and I did it.[12]

JAMES DRURY
*(*The Bleymier Story *and* The Cole Crawford Story*)*

The night I found out they wanted me for my first *Wagon Train (The Bleymier Story)*, I was in Utah on a fishing trip, in a remote location. I had no way of getting back to Los Angeles in time, so I charted a twin engine plane and was flown back to Burbank in a severe thunderstorm. I arrived at the studio twenty minutes before I was to begin work. I was disheveled from my trip, and desperately looked for a place to shower and shave. Just then, a resplendent gentleman dressed in a buckskin leather outfit approached me and said, "Mr. Drury, welcome to *Wagon Train.* My name is Bob Horton." He was genuinely gracious. I took from that a great lesson in how the star of a show could make a guest actor feel relaxed, comfortable, and function better. In one way or another, I adopted that rule on *The Virginian.* Interesting too that I had to get through a storm to do a script about one. They had rain machines on the set and we had water coming down on us the whole time we were filming.[13]

PAUL SAVAGE
(Executive Story Consultant: Gunsmoke*)*

I had known Howard Christie in the business, so I called him one day (during the latter part of the first season in March of 1958). I had an idea for an episode of *Wagon Train.* It involved this rough and tumble frontier woman who sets her sights on Major Seth Adams. I visualized Marjorie Main in the role, but I don't think she had done television. Howard's reaction was, "If I can get Marjorie to do TV, I'll do it." Fortunately, Howard had produced several of the *Ma and Pa Kettle* films at Universal that she starred in.

Well, Marjorie liked the idea and the story. I wrote the script and that was the origin of *The Cassie Tanner Story.*

Ward Bond was not that happy playing opposite such a broad, comedic character like Cassie. I think he envisioned himself as more of a latter-day John Wayne type, and this kind of deviated from that image. But Bond could play comedy, he went with it, and we captured a lot of the humor. It turned out to be a very well-done episode. Marjorie Main turned out to be an absolute princess of a lady. She was graciousness personified.[14]

Several characters first introduced in an episode made such an impression that they reappeared in later shows. Ernest Borgnine would reappear as Willie Moran in the opening episode of season two *(Around the Horn)*. Other characters from the first season such as Dora Gray (Linda Darnell), the vivacious con woman; Cliff Grundy (Dan Duryea), the colorful storyteller; as well as the aforementioned Cassie Tanner (Marjorie Main) all appeared in the season one finale *(The Sacramento Story)*. Other examples include Swift Cloud (Rafael Campos) who appeared during season two in the title role, and re-emerged the following season in *The Dr. Swift Cloud Story.* Samuel T. Evans (Mickey Rooney) whom we first met in *The Greenhorn Story* in season three, returned in *Wagons Ho!*, the opening show of season four. Kate Crawley (Barbara Stanwyck) who first appeared in the premier of season seven in *The Molly Kincaid Story*, returned later in the season in *The Kate Crawley Story.*

Numerous actors made several appearances throughout the series run including Rhonda Fleming, Dean Stockwell, Ann Blyth, Lee Marvin, Harry Carey, Jr., Noah Berry, Jr., J. Carrol Naish, Virginia Grey, Vera Miles, Joseph Cotton, Robert Ryan, Jack Warden, Leslie Nielsen, James Drury, Charles Drake, Neville Brand, Jan Sterling, Susan Oliver, Leonard Nimoy, Nancy Gates, Dana Wynter, Audrey Dalton, Michael Burns, Roger Mobley, Rory Calhoun, L.Q. Jones, Beverly Washburn, Read Morgan, Peter Brown, Carolyn Jones, Brandon DeWilde, Nick Adams, Jeanette Nolan, Greg Palmer, Gregory Walcott, Warren

Stevens, Anne Helm, Tommy Sands, James Lydon, Lory Patrick, William Smith, Diane Brewster, Jim Davis, Robert J. Wilke, and Morgan Woodward who appeared in twelve episodes.

The well-written stories and teleplays that attracted such a wide array of performers included such writers as Norman Jolley, Jean Holloway, Gene L. Coon, Allen Miner, Gerry Day, Leonard Praskins, John McGreevey, and initially by people such as William Fay, Dwight Newton, Robert Thompson, E. Jack Neuman, Aaron Spelling, and John Dunkel. Several guest stars also scripted episodes. Harry Von Zell wrote some very good shows. Gilbert Roland wrote the story for *The Bernal Sierra Story*, and Dana Wynter who guest starred in three episodes wrote the story for *The Lisa Raincloud Story*.

DANA WYNTER
(Guest Star: Multiple Episodes)

For me, at the time, westerns had been a form of entertainment with white hats vs. the black hats. I wasn't sure it went much deeper than that. I felt many of the women's roles seemed pedestrian and gutless with an emphasis on petticoats. To resolve that in my mind, I decided to write a character for myself and place it in the framework of a love story. At that time, I also thought about racism in America, so I incorporated that into the storyline to give it an added dimension. Lisa Raincloud was the daughter of a Caucasian woman that had married an Indian chief. A man from the wagon train (Bill Hawks) is wounded and brought to the village. Lisa nurses him back to health and they become attached. Hawks intends to marry Lisa but finds his wagon train family opposed to his plans. In reality, Lisa is not part Indian. Her biological father is not the Indian chief; so their prejudice is ill-founded. For Hawks the choice is equally heart-breaking on a different level. He's still very much part of a separate lifestyle, and can't leave it to make a new one with Lisa. I don't recall how much of my story was revised in the teleplay (which was written by Steven Ritch), but that was what I wrote and intended.[15]

At the outset of *Wagon Train*, the producer was Richard Lewis and the associate producer was Boris Ingster. Lewis helped to develop the series at Revue. However, the driving force behind the success and longevity of *Wagon Train* proved to be Howard Christie who had been producing films at Universal International. Christie produced the final 15 episodes of season one, beginning with *The Marie Dupree Story* which aired on March 25, 1958. At that point, Richard Lewis became the Executive Producer.

JOHN CHRISTIE
(Son of Howard Christie)

My father was a very kind considerate man, and a wonderful father. I don't ever remember him coming home angry or upset. He always came through the door with a smile. He loved what he did and the people that he worked with. He had his disputes at the studio but he was able to work them out in an amicable manner. I was told a story that illustrates that.

About the third year of the series, Ward Bond was feeling his oats as the star of the show. So one day he gets into a big argument with my father about Frank McGrath or Terry Wilson getting a salary increase. My father was a gentleman but I believe Bond was a bit relentless. At one point my father said, "Ward, this is none of your business. I'm the producer and I'll determine who gets a raise and who doesn't." Well, it went on for several days and finally my father decided that he had to put a stop to it. So he went to the wardrobe department and got an identical Ward Bond Wagonmaster outfit, complete with hat, holster and gun. He put it on, went to the set, walked up to Ward Bond and said, "Alright, if you wanna' be the producer, I'll be the wagonmaster." Bond broke up; and from then on, my father never had a problem being the producer or with Ward Bond being the wagonmaster.[16]

In the second season (1958–1959), Richard Lewis did not return. Frederick Shorr joined Howard Christie and became the associate producer, replacing Boris Ingster who also left the series.

FREDERICK SHORR
(Associate Producer 1958–1965)

Wagon Train was a very difficult show to make, but everyone involved worked very hard. We averaged 37 shows per season for the first five years I was with the series. Howard was a very good producer and much more creative than people gave him credit for. His concept was to do more personal stories on the show rather than make it a routine western. So we always looked for good stories based on character rather than action to make the show more of an anthology series. When *Wagon Train* first began, there were very few one-hour series on the air, so it became an important show to the network. We had to submit every script in advance to get approval from both NBC and the censors. I believe we had to have approval of every single person that worked on the show—both cast and crew. We had a lot of interesting relationships with a lot of people including Ward Bond, who was very right-wing, and I'm sure part of the approval process.[17]

JAMES LYDON
(Post-Production Supervisor
Revue Studios, 1962–1963)

Standards, practice and censorship were strict in 1950s and 1960s network television. An example was a 1962 episode of a popular Revue television series being previewed by a network representative. In one scene, a just-married couple ascended the stairs enroute to the bedroom. The network censor jumped up and said, "We can't show that. We'll lose our broadcast license." The sequence had to be re-done.[18]

Wagon Train was an ambitious effort from the start. During the first two seasons a lot of filming was done on location. Especially in the first year, that involved transporting Conestoga Wagons (sometimes close to a dozen or so would be used in a master shot), horses, oxen, and bus loads of extras, in addition to wranglers, stuntmen, cast, crew, and equipment.

JAMES H. BROWN
(First Assistant Director, 1958–1961)

In those days we usually didn't go to distant locations. We would drive out to places like Thousand Oaks and Janss Ranch, within 40 minutes of the studio, where you had plenty of rolling hills, oak trees, and could shoot in all directions. We also went to Iverson's Ranch where there were lots of rocks and sagebrush, and sometimes we'd go to Palmdale when we needed desert. We transported the wagons on flatbed trucks. A lot of them were four-ups (4 horses to a wagon), so early on, they would bring in sixty horses to accommodate a dozen Conestogas, the outriders, and cast, and use anywhere from thirty to forty extras; plus one wrangler for every five horses and one for each wagon team. As the show built up stock footage, we were able to use half as many wagons (sometimes as few as 3 or 4), and less of everything else, especially when the budget dictated so. But in the beginning, there was a huge investment made.[10]

The wranglers were an invaluable part of the show when it filmed on location. They not only took care of the horses but a number of them drove the wagons. That was an acquired skill, and a responsibility that was never given to an actor.

JAMES H. BROWN

We had a great bunch of tobacco-chewing old-timers that served as our wranglers on the series. Many of them were real cowboys who had driven stagecoaches to Yosemite prior to working in movies and television. It was easy to conceal a trained wrangler behind the actors sitting up front. They looked out through a slot in the wagon frame to guide the horses. On camera, the reins may have run through the actor's hands, but the horses were controlled by the "blind driver" behind them, who showed the actors what motions to make.[10]

Originally, the interiors for *Wagon Train* were filmed at Revue Studios (formerly Republic Studios and currently CBS Studio Center). The show was produced there for several seasons. When MCA became solely a producing entity and bought Universal, Revue moved to their lot at Universal City. (Revue became Universal in 1963.)

In the early days, each episode was given six days to film. As the series progressed, the studio tightened the budget and the shooting schedule was reduced to five days. The credo in television became to work fast, stay on schedule and do a good show.

JOE PEVNEY
(Director: Multiple Episodes 1958–1965)

When I began doing episodic television, I had come from directing feature films where you had much more time and a bigger budget. I was conditioned to that. One day, on the first episode I did, we were out on location. I had these wagons at the top of the hill and had them come all the way to the bottom. After we shot it, I wasn't satisfied, so I said, "Let's do it again." You should have heard the reaction from my crew. They stopped me cold. So I cut into one of the wagons and got the effect I wanted. Welcome to television.[19]

By the third and fourth season a pattern had been established. The bulk of location shooting was always done in the first 4–6 weeks of the season. (Footage from those shows plus stock shots accumulated from the previous two seasons were used throughout the year.) Most of the remaining shows were filmed on the soundstage at the studio with occasional exterior shots done on the back lot as needed.

DENNY SCOTT MILLER

We would shoot right there on the hill in back of Universal City. There was a lake on the opposite side of the hill and sometimes we'd shoot with that hill as the backdrop and be right next to the freeway. You could hardly hear the actor you were working with. You'd wait till their lips stopped moving and then you knew you were supposed to start talking. You knew you'd wind up looping (re-recording) your lines because of the extraneous noise.[20]

Shooting on a stage at the studio had lots of advantages. You never had to worry about losing light, or overhead clouds which might create problems in matching shots. You could do night scenes at any time of the day. There was no concern about overhead planes or extraneous noises when recording sound indoors. Rain, lightning, thunder and other effects could be easily created.

JAMES H. BROWN

We had a very large indoor set at the studio. On our stage, we had about 4–5 wagons positioned in a half-circle, plus a half-and-half (front and back) that we could use for cut-in pieces.

Behind the wagons were huge painted backdrops of rolling hills or desert with artificial sagebrush or cactus as needed. The campfires were fueled by propane. The camera's point of view gave you the illusion you were out in the wilderness. So we were able to do not only interiors but exteriors indoors.[10]

JAMES LYDON

The studio budget for Wagon Train was close to $100,000 per episode. The edict from Lew Wasserman (the head of the studio) was to get at least as much from the network per episode as it took to make. The studio made their profit on re-runs and syndication, not on first run airings of a show. That enabled the studio and filmed television to survive.[18]

Some interesting situations would occur on a sound stage, especially when animals were involved.

JOHN CHRISTIE

There was an episode in the fifth season called "Clyde" where Charlie Wooster finds a buffalo on the prairie, doesn't have the heart to shoot it, and brings it back to the wagon train. I have a distinct memory of these eight stagehands trying to secure it on the set. The buffalo wore this huge black collar with large rings on each side. Attached to the rings were small diameter cables with four men on each side holding onto them trying to secure the buffalo. The head on this buffalo was massive, and to cover up the collar for the camera, they had these huge brushes to comb the buffalo hair over the collar to hide it. When they'd get ready to shoot the scene, all of a sudden the buffalo would move his head to the right or left, and the four guys on the opposite side would slide across the floor like paper dolls.[16]

ROBERT HORTON

Toward the end of the third season, I decided to use my own horse on the show. He was an Appaloosa named Stormy Night. I had brought him down from Idaho in 1958, worked with him for a few years and he grew into a beautiful horse.

One day I was on him and we were on the stage doing a shot. A travois (litter) was attached behind him. I was transporting a woman from wherever I had rescued her. I rode into the scene, got off, helped the woman off the travois, then handed my horse to my stand-in who took him away. As he did, the side hook of the crossbar on the travois hooked itself on a wagon wheel. Stormy Night went berserk, ran to one end of the set and turned around. As he did, the travois (about 10-15 feet behind him) knocked people over like they were ten-pins. He then ran back toward the set and it looked like he was making a beeline for me. I leaped up on a wagon tongue as he came toward me. At that point, Terry (Wilson) who was a very strong man and knew a lot about horses, jumped on Stormy's head, threw his arms around his neck, eventually grabbed him by his ears and brought him to his knees. They undid the travois, Stormy got up, and everything was fine.[21]

As *Wagon Train* began its fourth year in the fall of 1960, the series was a well-established hit, firmly entrenched as the number two rated show in the Nielsen ratings.

Howard Christie was able to hire good directors who had a feel for the western, but no one imagined that the legendary John Ford would join the roster. Ford who had enjoyed a thirty-year friendship and association with John Wayne and Ward Bond, was never a man to mince words or refrain from voicing his opinion. After repeated criticism of *Wagon Train* scripts, Bond told Ford, "Jack, if you know so much, why don't you write one?" So he did. Ford wrote the story and had the script prepared by one of his writers. *The Colter Craven Story* aired on November 23, 1960. The story concerned Major Adams' efforts to rehabilitate an alcoholic doctor by giving him a chance to become a useful member of the wagon train. Carleton Young played the title role and a number of notable Ford stock players such as John Carradine, Anna Lee, Ken Curtis, Hank Worden, and Willis Bouchey were featured. John Wayne appeared as General William Tecumseh Sherman in a Civil War flashback sequence and was billed in the credits as Michael Morris.

JAMES H. BROWN

John Wayne was in one brief scene. He walked his horse into the shot, delivered his line, got off, said another line, then got back on his horse and exited frame. Ford shot him in darkness and back lit the scene. Unless you knew it was John Wayne, you couldn't recognize him. But even in silhouette and slumped in his saddle, he was an imposing figure with a tremendous presence. It was something to see.[10]

GARY YOGGY

The Colter Craven Story was one of the finest episodes in the series. Major Adams inspires Craven to sober up enough to perform a serious operation by telling him the story of how General Ulysses S. Grant (depicted as a close friend of Adams) was dismissed from the U.S. Army for alcoholism, but later re-instated, allowing him to lead the Union forces to victory and propel him into the White House. Ford presents this "great American story" in a way that makes Grant's disgrace an inspiration and his weakness the cowardly doctor's opportunity for redemption.[2]

On the surface it appeared John Ford was not a fan of the television medium. "You can't build a scene the way you can in a movie. There's no time to do it," he'd say. "If you want to re-write something, by the time you find the writer, you're into next week's segment." But in reality, Ford enjoyed a certain kinship with *Wagon Train.* He loved the western genre and was a highly efficient director who got things done; so the time constraints imposed by the studio were not a deterrent. In fact, Revue gave him an extra day to shoot his script. In six days, Ford shot 72 minutes of quality films, far more than most television directors were required to do. The studio was so impressed they thought of making it into a two-parter; but eventually edited it down to the acceptable length of about 52 minutes.

L. Q. JONES

One day, Frank McGrath and I are playin' "Pitch" (a card game) on the stage when John Ford comes in. He was pre-parin' to shoot an episode of *Wagon Train* (with the Duke). Frank sees him and says, "Hey, you've never worked for Ford, have ya'?" I said "No" and Frank says, "Well, I'll take care of that." I said, "No, don't go…" and Frank says, "Don't worry. Everything is fine." So he goes over to Ford and when he gets done, I'm a combination of Clark Gable, Spencer Tracy and God knows who else. Frank comes back and says, "It's all taken care of." We resume playin' and ten minutes later, Ford starts to go. Frank runs over to him before he can get out the door , then comes back, gets me and takes me over to meet him. Well, Ford is standin' there with one hand on the door. He sizes me up from head to toe, takes a second look at me, and has the most disgusted look on his face, as if he caught this ripe aroma, but not quite sure from where. When I saw the expression on his face, I began to laugh. I thought it was funny. Ford didn't think so. He stormed out and he never spoke to me again. I guess I never should have laughed, but it wouldn't have made a difference. I probably would have said something smart the first day we worked together, or he would have, I would have come back at him and he would have fired me. But God, I would loved to have worked with the old man![5]

On November 5, 1960, Ward Bond suffered a fatal heart attack while making a personal appearance in Texas. He was 57 years old. Seven episodes had already aired that fourth season, and Bond was seen intermittently in five more shows through February 22, 1961 when he made his final appearance in *The Beth Pearson Story.*

ROBERT HORTON

The night before Ward went to Texas for the weekend, I dropped by his dressing room. I had issues with a script that I wanted to share with him. After we talked I said, "Ward, I know we've had our differences, but we both agree this is a terrible script." He placed his hand on my shoulder and said, "Bobby" (he had never called me Bobby before), "we don't have any differences." I smiled, said good night, walked out and that was the last time I saw him.[3]

GARY YOGGY

In *The Beth Pearson Story*, Major Adams is shaken by the resemblance of Beth, a widow traveling with her son on the train, to the late Ranie Webster, a woman he once loved and wanted to marry. (*The Major Adams Story, Part One* and *Part Two*, 4/23/58 and 4/30/58). Seth Adams finds himself falling in love again. Beth Pearson wants him to be certain it is she, and not the memory of the dead woman that he is in love with. After a tragic accident in which Mrs. Pearson breaks her neck and almost dies, Adams realizes that he is still in love with Ranie's ghost and he cannot marry Beth. (Virginia Grey, who had played Ranie Webster in the earlier episodes, is cast as Beth Pearson.) A decision had been made not to explain the absence of Seth Adams from the series, but loyal fans could rationalize his absence by assuming that after his ghostly experience with love, he was so emotionally drained that he decided to leave the train and take life easy, or perhaps even search out Beth Pearson whom he's decided he really did love after all.[2]

ROBERT HORTON

After Ward's passing, there was talk about me taking over the role of wagonmaster. I was very much against it. I thought it should be played by an older man. I also felt that part of Flint McCullough's appeal was that he accepted responsibility when he chose to. He had never gotten into a situation where he was tied down. He was independent and very much a loner.

I did do four episodes which were written for Ward, but I did them because Howard (Christie) was in a bind. I can remember one show that contradicted what I had established as my character. The writers simply took Major Adams out of the script and put in Flint McCullough over his speeches. The story involved a woman being dragged off by the Indians. By the time it was cut and edited, it looked as if I stood by and made no effort to prevent it. Now with an older man in that situation, his physical limitations would prevent him from doing anything. Or with Ward in the role, with his knowledge and maturity, he'd say "There's nothing to be done" and you'd believe it. But when Flint stood by in the prime of his life and did nothing, it invalidated his image.[22]

On March 16, 1961, three weeks after Ward Bond's final appearance, with fourteen episodes remaining in the season, John McIntire was introduced as the new wagonmaster in *The Christopher Hale Story*.

McIntire, 54 at the time, came by the part naturally. His father was a frontier lawyer, rancher, and long-time commissioner of Indian Affairs in Montana where McIntire grew up.

He became an actor when he majored in speech at the University of Southern California and got into radio announcing shortly after. Eventually he began to work in movies and appeared in dozens of westerns. Some of his best roles were in Anthony Mann films such as *Winchester 73* and *Night Passage*. His wife, Jeanette Nolan, was a skillful character actress in her own right.

As Chris Hale, McIntire's on-screen persona was much different than that of Ward Bond's Seth Adams. Hale was more educated and philosophical, less a disciplinarian, and gentler but not soft. Where Major Adams could be loud and bellowing, Chris Hale would be cool and calm.

ROBERT HORTON

I was delighted when they picked John McIntire to be the new wagonmaster. In fact, I had suggested him for two guest roles that season. John was a versatile actor and my kind of performer.[22]

L. Q. JONES

John was one of the best character actors in the business and I always enjoyed working with both him and Jeannie (Jeanette Nolan). In one of the *Wagon Train* episodes I did (*Charlie Wooster-Outlaw*), Jeannie played this lady outlaw with Morgan Woodward and me as her two sons. In the story, we're supposed to kidnap John (Chris Hale) but grab Frank (Charlie Wooster) by mistake. It was a comedy directed by Virgil Vogel.

Well, we're sailin' along, we get to the final day of shooting, Virgil starts fallin' behind and he's beside himself. It's late in the day. We're already on "golden time" (double overtime) and he says, "We're gonna' have to break for dinner, then come back and finish this. We've got another three to four hours of work here." No one wanted to hear that. Everyone wanted to go home. Before we broke, I sat down, took everything we had to do, put it together in one camera move and showed it to Virgil. He thought it would never work but agreed to try it. It was a very funny sequence. So we shot it, it worked and everyone was hysterical. We were also done and out of there in less than an hour.

After we did that show, every time Virgil got a job he asked for me. It got to a point where he wouldn't take no for an answer. One time he was doing a *Big Valley* but they couldn't afford my price. In this particular show, Virgil had two cameras because a lot of it took place in a courtroom. So Virgil did away with one of the cameras to get enough money to hire me. I must have worked for him fifteen times.[5]

MORGAN WOODWARD
(Appeared in twelve episodes)
That particular *Wagon Train* show turned out so well that there was talk about a "spin-off series" with Jeanette as the outlaw Bella McKavitch, and L. Q. and I as her two sons. I believe they began to develop the project, but it never came to fruition. Regardless, we loved working for Howard Christie. He was a wonderful producer and I was always appreciative of the fact that he had confidence in my ability, and cast me in a variety of roles.[23]

On January 25, 1961 in the 19th episode of season four entitled *Weight of Command*, Denny Miller appeared as Duke Shannon, an assistant scout hired by Major Adams.

Miller was a tall, blonde, blue-eyed basketball player from UCLA. He was placed under contract to Revue Studios the day after he graduated. Miller appeared in a number of TV shows at Revue such as *Overland Trail, Laramie, Riverboat*, and *The Deputy* before joining *Wagon Train*. Miller was genuine and likeable, and Ward Bond encouraged the studio to bring Miller back.

Miller was officially introduced twelve episodes later on April 26 in *The Duke Shannon Story*. However, they weren't pleased with his name.

DENNY SCOTT MILLER
I was twenty-four and used to it. It fit me. I didn't want to change it and I told them so. The studio claimed Denny didn't sound manly or mature. They said that first

names ending in "y" weren't right for leading men. What about Jimmy Stewart, Henry Fonda, or Tony Curtis? Well, they dropped that line of thought but didn't give up. So this is how we settled on it. I said I wouldn't change my last name. My folks had named me in the first place, so they would come up with a list of ten first names. I gave the studio the list and they picked Scott. My billing on *Wagon Train* was "Denny Miller" at the start, "Denny Scott Miller" for a while, and finally "Scott Miller." When I left *Wagon Train*, I went back to "Denny Miller."[11]

Although Bond was gone, Robert Horton and John McIntire accepted Miller and were helpful to him.

DENNY SCOTT MILLER

I was very fortunate. I was inserted into the cast of a hit television series, yet I was inexperienced. A stranger in a strange land. Bob (Horton) and John (McIntire) were kind to me and did their best to put me at ease. As the show wore on, Terry and Frank became my friends and guided me through it. *Wagon Train* was my schooling and the cast became my mentors. Terry and Frank were two of the best stuntmen in the business. They were dependable, professional, all the good things. Terry had a quiet strength about him which was reassuring. In *The Duke Shannon Story* he and I did one of the best fight scenes ever on TV (according to Lew Wasserman). We ended up facing each other, both on our knees, too weak to stand up but still strong enough to punch each other.[20]

During the fourth season, Robert Horton grew dissatisfied with the direction of the series. He felt that the show no longer had the scope and flow it once had, due to increasing studio economy.

ROBERT HORTON

Ward had this huge ad or clipping in his dressing room that stated Revue had made 39 million dollars on *Wagon Train*. His comment, penciled in underneath was: "Then what's all this ____ ____ talk about cutting the budget?" We were both in there fighting the studio about that.[22]

Wagon Train, in fact, had undergone some change. The show went on location far less frequently than it did in the first two seasons due to the accumulation of stock footage. Horton felt a number of the scripts had become "soft and talky," and that his character was increasingly placed in scripts where there was no relationship between his job as scout and the other characters.

Despite the conflicts and distractions that arose, along with a slightly diminished presence that season (due to scripts he asked to be written out of), Horton gave strong performances in episodes like *The River Crossing*, *The Earl Packard Story* and *The Odyssey of Flint McCullough* which showcased his compassion and thoughtfulness as an actor.

ROBERT HORTON

The Odyssey of Flint McCullough was basically a story about five children and the effect they have on Flint. I enjoyed it because it called on all the relationships a man can have with children when he wants to trust them as equals and get them to feel a part of something and their responsibility as people. I got the chance to advocate for an Indian youth and express my feelings about minority problems and other things I felt strongly about.[22]

However, without Ward Bond, there was something missing from the show.

ROBERT HORTON

Ward's character was so well-established and the relationship of Major Adams and Flint McCullough so worthwhile that we could make just about anything work, even when there wasn't much of a story to tell.[3]

At that point, Horton decided to move in another direction.

ROBERT HORTON

Toward the end of the fourth season in the spring of 1961, I decided I would leave the series at the end of the fifth year when my contract was up. I had always enjoyed singing. My wife Marilynn was a concert singer who had a scholarship to the New England Conservatory of Music and she was very encouraging. I began to study voice regularly and my interest grew very strong in that area. During my hiatus time from *Wagon Train*, I did *Guys and Dolls* (with Marilynn) in Ohio, and *Brigadoon* in Connecticut. In my spare time I read musical scripts, and after I left the show, I set my sights on working in musical theater and doing Broadway.

I wasn't turning my back on doing another series. I liked television and was grateful for the success it afforded me. At the same time, I felt tired, restless and unchallenged. I wanted to try another medium. I felt I was young enough to go work in the theater, and if I were fortunate, come back at some point and do another TV series.[2, 22]

During the fifth season (1961–1962) Horton starred in ten episodes while Denny Scott Miller starred in eight. Horton left the series in the spring of 1962, when *Wagon Train* was the number one rated show in the country. The studio tried everything to keep him, offering Horton a very lucrative ten-year contract, plus a percentage of *Wagon Train*, but to no avail.

Ironically, Horton's departure, too, was never explained. Flint McCullough rode away at the end of *The Nancy Davis Story* on May 16, 1962 and was never seen or heard from again.

The producers, cast and crew opted to give Horton a farewell party on the set, but the studio forbade it. They wanted to minimize all forms of publicity with regard to his leaving.

FREDERICK SHORR

When Bob decided to leave the series, Lew Wasserman (the studio's Chairman of the Board) was very anxious to keep him. We were the number one show on television. Bob had a huge following and had been a vital part of *Wagon Train*; but he was adamant about leaving. Unfortunately, that was something that happens on a lot of television series when the star chooses to go on to something else.[17]

With the loss of Robert Horton, *Wagon Train* was not renewed by NBC for a sixth year. ABC picked up the show for the 1962–1963 season and placed it in the same time slot on Wednesday nights. John McIntire continued his duties as wagonmaster Chris Hale, with Denny Scott Miller as lone Scout Duke Shannon, and Terry Wilson and Frank McGrath as assistant wagonmaster and cook, respectively.

In its sixth year and first on ABC, *Wagon Train* dropped from number one to number 25 in the Nielsen's. Opposite them in their former time slot on NBC was a new 90-minute western series, *The Virginian*, filmed in color, and also produced at Revue. The show starred James Drury in the title role, with Lee J. Cobb as Judge Garth, Doug McClure as Trampas, Gary Clarke as Steve, and Roberta Shore as Betsy Garth. To compete with *The Virginian*, and breathe new life into *Wagon Train's* seventh season, ABC moved it to Monday nights, expanded it to 90 minutes, and ordered 32 episodes filmed in color.

Robert Fuller who had starred in the popular NBC western *Laramie* (another Revue production) was brought in to play *Wagon Train* scout Cooper Smith alongside Duke Shannon.

Fuller had first appeared on *Wagon Train* in the second season with Betty Davis in *The Ella Lindstrom Story* then returned to deliver a strong guest performance in *The Kate Parker Story* opposite Virginia Grey, Warren Stevens and Ruta Lee.

ROBERT FULLER
(Cooper Smith 1963–1965)

The day I found out *Laramie* was going to end, Patrick Kelly (who was V.P. in charge of talent at Revue) called me in and asked if I would like to go into *Wagon Train*. I didn't have to think twice about going from one western to another; and working with John, Denny, Terry and Frank was more than okay with me.[24]

Another new addition to the cast was teenager Michael Burns as Barnaby West. The character had been established in the final episode of season six *(The Barnaby West Story)* when the thirteen-year-old had come west by himself in an attempt to find his father.

Burns was a well-adjusted teenager who was naturally talented. He had acted in a number of network TV shows, and prior to being introduced as Barnaby, Burns made five appearances on *Wagon Train* including *The Jeremy Dow Story*, *The Odyssey of Flint McCullough* and *The Dr. Denker Story*.

With the addition of contrasting lead Fuller and teenager Burns in an expanded format, ABC hoped to broaden the show's audience appeal and boost the ratings.

HARRY FLYNN
(ABC Publicist 1962–1964)
It was more expensive to film in color when you factored in the cost of cameras, lighting, lab work and the time it took to coordinate the color process. But the end result was the studio did a good job of filming the color episodes. It was hard to tell the difference between the interior campfire scenes shot on the sound stage and the exteriors filmed on location.[25]

DENNY SCOTT MILLER
When we went to color, we all thought we'd look great in buckskin. So we went to the wardrobe department and had them make our outfits from buckskin. They didn't tell us that color film required three times as much light as black-and-white. It became so hot, it felt like being in a sauna. In the second week, we were back at wardrobe asking for our cotton shirts back. The only other adjustment for me was my blue eyes getting used to the lights. When we shot outside with reflector boards and huge klieg lights, my eyes would tear up. But after a while, I squinted a lot and eventually looked like the only blonde Chinese cowboy.[20]

To take advantage of filming in color, the *Wagon Train* company traveled to Lone Pine, California and Kanab, Utah.

DENNY SCOTT MILLER
Lone Pine is an impressive location about 200 miles north of Los Angeles. It's at the base of Mt. Whitney and at times you see snow in the background. They filmed a lot of the *Hopalong Cassidy* westerns there and it remains unchanged and has maintained its character through the years. We did a color episode there with Peter Falk and Tommy Sands.[20]

TOMMY SANDS
(Guest Star: Multiple Episodes)
Lone Pine was a beautiful place with a lot of movie western history. I remember we were shooting up in the mountains and I was affected by the altitude change. I began to get short of breath and I called my wife Nancy to come and stay with

me. Ironically at one point in the script, my character collapses from exhaustion, and I didn't have to do much acting in that scene.[26]

DENNY SCOTT MILLER

The beauty of shooting in Kanab, Utah was that within a short distance, you had cliffs, mountains, flat plains, streams and forest. We had great community support there. Kanab was promoted as a location for movie and TV companies so they accepted us with open arms. It was such a boon to their economy.[20]

Wagon Train filmed a lot of new color footage in Utah for their seventh season. On one occasion, a busload of extras were brought in, and various shots were filmed of the travelers coming around the mountain, through the woods, crossing the stream, using 3 to 4 wagons with camera angles, giving the illusion of more Conestogas behind them. They repeated this process in every location they went to, always shooting right to left. (This was due to the fact that if you look on a map and pointed toward California, you'd be traveling right to left.)

Robert Fuller was an actor who loved being involved in a lot of the scenes being filmed even when he wasn't a part of them.

DENNY SCOTT MILLER

There was a scene in Kanab where we needed Indians for a raiding party. So we used every Indian kid we could find in the nearby high school. The problem was a lot of them couldn't ride, and as they came down the hill blinded by red clay dust, they fell off their horses and got hurt. Bob came to work that afternoon and saw the number of Indians had dwindled. So he put on an Indian wig and costume, jumped on a horse and joined the raiding party. He probably rode in about three shots before the director, William Witney, became aware of it. Witney didn't approve. He couldn't have one of his stars risking injury. So he got on the bullhorn and called Bob in. But Bob wouldn't come in. So Witney walked all the way out to where the raiding party was, found the Indian he thought was Bob and proceeded to tell him what he thought of him.

The problem was, it wasn't Bob. Bob was behind the guy on horseback, watching the whole thing.[20]

Fuller never confined his actions to television. He did it in movies too. When they filmed *Spartacus* at the studio, he participated in one of the battle scenes.

ROBERT FULLER

One time on *Laramie*, I spent the whole morning working with Rod Cameron who was a good friend of mine. I finished at noon. So I went back to the set that afternoon, made up with a beard, wearing different clothes and a hat. I worked alongside Rod in this barroom scene half the afternoon. He never knew it was me. Neither did the director.[24]

The 90-minute episodes attracted a lot of top notch guest stars for several reasons. The expanded time length gave license to tell a decent story, develop the characters, and provide a good showcase for the actors.

DENNY SCOTT MILLER

Wagon Train was instrumental in breaking down the caste system. The highest caste were those actors that had achieved stardom in movies, and felt television at that time was beneath them. However, Howard Christie and Fred Shorr provided us with such wonderful stories about individuals, that they named the shows after them and paid the actors accordingly. As a result, a lot of big-name guest stars appeared on *Wagon Train*. It became acceptable to appear and guest star in an episodic television show. The opposite was also true. Television created a number of movie stars like Steve McQueen, James Garner, and Clint Eastwood who got their start in TV.[20]

ROBERT FULLER

Rhonda Fleming was one of the most beautiful women in the world and she did several of our shows. She guest-starred in a 90-minute *Wagon Train* I did, and when she came on the set she was a lovely lady. She played a dance hall singer. One day we had this scene that took place in her dressing room after she had performed. She was wearing a very low-cut dance outfit, and Rhonda was very well endowed. It was about a 2 1/2 page scene. We shot it and it went well—I thought.

The next day Howard Christie came down on the set and asked me to come up and look at dailies (from yesterday) when I had a break. I went up to the projection room and it was Howard, Fred and myself. They ran the scene I did with Rhonda. Well, as the scene goes on, you see that Rhonda is looking into my eyes, but I'm not looking into hers. I'm looking straight down at her chest. It was very obvious, and unbelievable that no one saw or picked up on it when we did the scene. I said, "Oh, my God. What do you want to do?" And Howard said, "We have to shoot it over." I said, "Well, what are you gonna' tell Rhonda?" "I'm going to tell her the truth," said Howard. I said, "No, you can't do that." But they did and she thought it was great. We shot the scene over and it was fine.[24]

When *Wagon Train* returned for its eighth season, the show underwent more changes. Denny Scott Miller did not return, leaving Robert Fuller as the lone scout. The ratings dropped for the second straight year. In an effort to counteract that, ABC moved the show to Sunday nights at 7:30 P.M. However, the decline in ratings couldn't justify filming 90-minute episodes in color; so the show returned to the one-hour format in black and white. Twenty six episodes were filmed in what turned out to be the final year.

After eight seasons, nearly 700 guest stars, over 12,000 actors, and 4000 horses, *Wagon Train* reached California and did not return to St. Joseph, Missouri for an encore trip.

In retrospect, the television and movie westerns made years ago were much different than those made today.

PETER BROWN
(Guest Star: Multiple Episodes)

When I look at some of the old westerns, it's hard to imagine you could improve on films like *Ride the High Country*, *The Searchers*, and *Red River*. I recently watched a video of *The Big Trail* with "Duke" Wayne, directed by Raoul Welsh. That had to be one of the best westerns ever made in terms of ambition and authenticity. There were scenes where they were lowering Conestoga wagons down 300 foot cliffs by rope, block and tackle; where someone was swimming across a river with a six-month infant in their arms. They could never duplicate that today. The industry wouldn't allow it.[27]

WARREN STEVENS
(Guest Star: Multiple Episodes)

Many of those older westerns, including the stories on *Wagon Train*, were morality tales. There were relationships between the principal characters on screen that you understood and appreciated, with far less emphasis on superfluous action and detail.[28]

DEBRA PAGET

I really loved the old westerns. They're part of Americana. However, the world is different today, and I'm not sure they could make them now the way they did then. I remember some of the westerns I did in the 1950s, like *Broken Arrow*, for example. The action in the film never got in the way of character development. You never lost sight of the story. I think that's what's missing in today's westerns. There's too much emphasis on violence. In the older westerns on television and in films, much of that occurred off-camera. It allowed you to use your imagination and that was just as effective.[9]

DIANE FOSTER
(Guest Star: Multiple Episodes)

I think today the people are looking for heroes. We don't have the strong, fearless tough guys like John Wayne that you admired and looked up to. They don't exist anymore. The heroes in the westerns of days-gone-by may have had flaws, but they still had a redeeming nature, and there was some connection between them and the audience. I see many movies today where I don't like any of the characters in the story. There doesn't seem to be time given to the characters to explain who they are and allow you to get close to them. Instead, the accent is on violence and gore.[29]

MORGAN WOODWARD

I think a lot of the actors today don't understand the western genre, and they can't do a genuine dialect. Back when we were doing westerns, a lot of actors understood the cowboy culture and were able to pick up the proper behavior and self-expression. We also had good directors that understood the western folkways. Today it's very different and you don't find many people like that; and it's reflected in the moviemaking.[23]

ROBERT FULLER

In 1960 there were about 32 westerns in prime time. There were lots of directors that knew how to shoot them, writers who knew their western history, and actors who understood the cowboy and his way of life. There were also probably 600 horses that were trained to work in films and television. They could run, go up and down hills, lope, move or stand still when they had to. You could shoot a Winchester or a .45 over their head and it wouldn't bother them. You couldn't find horses like that today. They're just not around. Neither are the actors who rode them, the directors who filmed them or the writers who wrote about them. I did a western some years back where we got on location and the only horses available were cow horses. They weren't trained for film and it was difficult. They wanted to chase cows; not stand still in front of the camera when they had to. On another occasion, I was supposed to ride up a mountain shooting a Winchester in an action sequence. Before I rode out to the location, I said to the head wrangler, "Has anyone shot off this horse before?" He said, "I don't think so." I got off the horse and they spent half a day working with him to get him ready so I could climb back on and fire without getting thrown off. That's an example of what's become of the business today.

So when I look back at *Wagon Train*, *Laramie*, and all the other western films and television I was fortunate to do, I feel blessed.[24]

So do the people that watched *Wagon Train*. It became more than a weekly television western about people traveling to California. Each episode reflected human emotion of the pioneers that was universal, and by setting those hardships against a backdrop of the western frontier, they became all the more defined and memorable to the millions of people that grew up watching the show.

WARD BOND enjoyed a prolific career as a supporting actor in feature films before becoming a huge television star on NBC's *Wagon Train*.

FLINT McCULLOUGH (Robert Horton) and **MAJOR SETH ADAMS** (Ward Bond) see trouble brewing at the outset of their journey in an early *Wagon Train* episode in the fall of 1957.

GEORGE MONTGOMERY, PENNY EDWARDS and **ROBERT HORTON** on location during filming of *The Jesse Cowan Story* shown January 8th, 1958. Montgomery would star the following season on network television in Cimarron City co-starring John Smith and Audrey Totter.

FLINT McCULLOUGH (Robert Horton) and DORA GRAY (Linda Darnell) encounter opposition on their way to an army fort in *The Dora Gray Story,* during Season One on January 29, 1958.

FLINT McCULLOUGH (Robert Horton) SETH ADAMS (Ward Bond) and CHARLIE WOOSTER (Frank McGrath) see signs of an impending uprising in a 1958 first season episode.

ROBERT HORTON greets **GILBERT ROLAND** (who played his father in the MGM film *Apache War Smoke*) on the set of *The Bernal Sierra Story*. Roland wrote the story for the episode which aired March 12, 1958.

Homeless drifter TOBIAS JONES (Lou Costello) and orphan MIDGE (Beverly Washburn) share a moment of crisis in *The Tobias Jones Story,* the fourth episode of Season Two, shown October 22,1958.

TOBIAS JONES (Lou Costello) tries to explain his innocence to MAJOR ADAMS (Ward Bond). The script was written by Harry Von Zell, and was the only dramatic appearance Costello ever made on film.

PENNY DAVIS (Evelyn Rudie) shares an affectionate moment with her mother's friend **FLINT McCULLOUGH (Robert Horton)** in *The Millie Davis Story,* broadcast November 26, 1958.

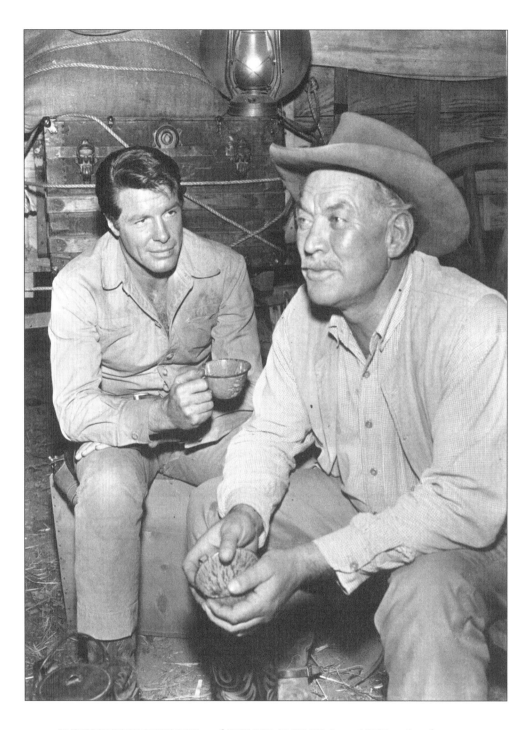

ROBERT HORTON and **WARD BOND** in a 1959 episode. They were two contrasting personalities who enjoyed a wonderful rapport on camera. Their on-screen chemistry solidified the series and made *Wagon Train* a grand success.

ROBERT HORTON sweeps veteran actress **JANE DARWELL** off her feet during filming of *The Vivian Carter Story*, telecast March 11,1959 during season two.

BETTY DAVIS points something out to actress **MAGGIE PIERCE** on the set of *The Elizabeth McQueeny Story*. The show aired during the third season on October 28, 1959. Davis guest starred in two other episodes: *The Ella Lindstrom Story* (Season Two) and *The Betina May Story* (Season Five).

ROBERT HORTON with his Appaloosa **STORMY NIGHT.**
He began to ride him on the show at the end of Season Three in
the spring of 1960.

MAJOR ADAMS (Ward Bond) leads the wagon train across the prarie at the outset of the fourth season in the fall of 1960.

A behind the scenes look at filming of *The Bleymier Story* in October of 1960, where FLINT McCULLOUGH (Robert Horton) is confronted by prophet of doom SAMUEL BLEYMIER (Dan Duryea). Said actor James Drury who also appeared in the episode: "They had rain machines on the set and we had water coming down on us the whole time we filmed."

Academy Award winning master **JOHN FORD** directs **WARD BOND** in *The Colter Craven Story,* which featured a cameo appearance by **JOHN WAYNE**. Ford was undeterred by TV's fast pace and shot 72 minutes of film in six days, with about 20 minutes of extra footage.

FLINT McCULLOUGH (Robert Horton) greets former
girlfriend ALLISON JUSTIS (Gloria DeHaven) unaware that
a horse thief he shot was her husband. *The Allison Justis Story*
aired October 19, 1960 during the Fourth Season.

DENNY SCOTT MILLER first appeared as **DUKE SHANNON** during the Fourth Season episode *Weight of Command*. Genuine, likeable, and hardworking, Miller impressed Ward Bond who lobbied the producers to bring Miller back. Three months later, he was formally introduced in *The Duke Shannon Story* in April of 1961, and remained with the show for over three years.

TERRY WILSON who portrayed ramrod and assistant wagon-master **BILL HAWKS** was once a top stunt man in the motion picture industry.

New wagonmaster JOHN McINTIRE with ROBERT
HORTON in June of 1961.

FRANK McGRATH *(opposite)* celebrates a birthday on
February 3, 1961 on the set of *The Tiburcio Mendez Story,* and
receives a congratulatory kiss from guest star LISA GAYE. The
show also featured Nehemiah Persoff in the title role along with
Leonard Nimoy.

DANA WYNTER and **DENNY SCOTT MILLER** during filming of *The Lizabeth Ann Calhoun Story* shown December 6, 1961 during Season Five.

DUKE SHANNON (Denny Scott Miller) protects con man
MALACHI HOBART (Franchot Tone) from an assault in
The Malachi Hobart Story on January 24,1962.

**FLINT McCULLOUGH (Robert Horton) struggles to free a
wagon in** *Swamp Devil,* **the 27th episode of the Fifth Season on
April 4, 1962.**

JOHN and **CHRISTINE CHRISTIE** visit the *Wagon Train* set in 1962.

After five seasons, **ROBERT HORTON** left the series in May of 1962. At the time, *Wagon Train* was the top-rated show in the country. The studio tried everything imaginable to keep him, but to no avail. Three years later after appearing on Broadway and in regional theaters throughout the country, Horton returned to star in ABC's *A Man Called Shenandoah*.

In Sacramento, **CHARLIE WOOSTER** (Frank McGrath)
BILL HAWKS (Terry Wilson) and **DUKE SHANNON** (Denny
Scott Miller) look on as wagonmaster **CHRIS HALE** (John
McIntire) is smitten with **HEATHER MAHONEY** (Jane Wyatt).
The Heather Mahoney Story was the final episode of the Fifth
Season. It aired June 13, 1962.

TERRY WILSON, JOHN McINTIRE, FRANK McGRATH
and **DENNY SCOTT MILLER** (on horseback in background)
on location at Red Rock Canyon in 1962.

MAVIS GRANT (Ann Sheridan) proves to be inhospitable to **CHRIS HALE** and his travelers in *The Mavis Grant Story* shown October 24, 1962 during Season Six.

Actress **DANA WYNTER** on location in the title role of
The Lisa Raincloud Story. Wynter wrote the story for the
episode which aired October 31, 1962.

DUKE SHANNON, BILL HAWKS and **CHRIS HALE** lead the wagon train across rugged terrain in 1963.

ROBERT FULLER joined the *Wagon Train* cast as scout **COOPER SMITH** for the Seventh Season in the fall of 1963. The series expanded to 90 minutes and 32 episodes were filmed in color.

MICHAEL BURNS first appeared as teenager **BARNABY WEST** in the last episode of the Sixth Season and joined the cast of the series for the final two years.

BARBARA STANWYCK as freight operator KATE CRAWLEY
in *The Molly Kincaid Story*, the lead-off episode of *Wagon Train's*
Seventh Season, September 16, 1963. She reprised her role four
months later in *The Kate Crawley Story* on January 27, 1964.

CHRIS HALE (John McIntire), DUKE SHANNON (Denny Scott Miller) and BARNABY WEST (Michael Burns) in a 1963 promotion photo.

CHRIS HALE (John McIntire) and COOPER SMITH (Robert Fuller) in December of 1963.

DUKE SHANNON (Denny Scott Miller) confronts MRS. CARTER (Joanna Moore) in *The Duncan McIvor Story*, shown March 9, 1964.

The *Wagon Train* cast in the summer of 1964 as filming begins for the eighth and final season. The show returned to the one hour format and was filmed in black and white.

BROADCAST HISTORY & CAST (1957-1965)

BROADCAST HISTORY

NBC	Wednesday Nights	7:30 P.M.–8:30 P.M.	(1957–1962)
ABC	Wednesday Nights	7:30 P.M.–8:30 P.M.	(1962–1963)
ABC	Monday Nights	8:30 P.M.–10:00 P.M.	(1963–1964)
ABC	Sunday Nights	7:30 P.M.–8:30 P.M.	(1964–1965)

THE CAST

Major Seth Adams	Ward Bond	(1957–1961)
Flint McCullough	Robert Horton	(1957–1962)
Bill Hawks	Terry Wilson	(1957–1965)
Chuck Wooster	Frank McGrath	(1957–1965)
Duke Shannon	Denny Scott Miller	(1961–1964)
Chris Hale	John McIntire	(1961–1965)
Cooper Smith	Robert Fuller	(1963–1965)
Barnaby West	Michael Burns	(1963–1965)

WAGON TRAIN
Season One: 1957-1958

Episode Titles	Air Dates
1. The Willy Moran Story	9/18/57
2. The Jean LeBec Story	9/25/57
3. The John Cameron Story	10/2/57
4. The Ruth Owens Story	10/9/57
5. The Les Rand Story	10/16/57
6. The Nels Stack Story	10/23/57
7. The Emily Rossiter Story	10/30/57
8. The John Darro Story	11/6/57
9. The Charles Avery Story	11/13/57
10. The Mary Halstead Story	11/20/57
11. The Zeke Thomas Story	11/27/57
12. The Riley Gratton Story	12/4/57
13. The Clara Beauchamp Story	12/11/57
14. The Julia Gage Story	12/18/57
15. The Cliff Grundy Story	12/25/57
16. The Luke O'Malley Story	1/1/58
17. The Jesse Cowan Story	1/8/58
18. The Gabe Carswell Story	1/15/58
19. The Honorable Don Charlie Story	1/22/58
20. The Dora Gray Story	1/29/58
21. The Annie MacGregor Story	2/5/58
22. The Bill Tawnee Story	2/12/58
23. The Mark Hanford Story	2/26/58
24. The Bernal Sierra Story	3/12/58
25. The Marie Dupree Story	3/19/58

Episode Titles	*Air Dates*
26. A Man Called Horse	3/26/58
27. The Sarah Drummond Story	4/2/58
28. The Sally Potter Story	4/9/58
29. The Daniel Barrister Story	4/16/58
30. The Major Adams Story (1)	4/23/58
31. The Major Adams Story (2)	4/30/58
32. The Charles Maury Story	5/7/58
33. The Dan Hogan Story	5/14/58
34. The Ruttledge Munroe Story	5/21/58
35. The Rex Montana Story	5/28/58
36. The Cassie Tanner Story	6/4/58
37. The John Wilbot Story	6/11/58
38. The Monty Britton Story	6/18/58
39. The Sacramento Story	6/25/58

#1. The Willy Moran Story
Written by: William Fay & William Cox
Directed by: Herschel Daugherty

In St. Joseph, Missouri, with the wagon train about to roll, Major Seth Adams rescues Willy Moran with whom he served in the Civil War. Moran, once a great fighter, is now an alcoholic, unable to earn an honest living. Adams offers Moran a job on the train as a driver for a traveler named Robinson, but warns him not to drink during the trip west.

When a young widow on the train shows interest in Moran, he hopes to redeem himself. However, Robinson finds more use for him as a drunkard.

Willy Moran (Ernest Borgnine), *Mary Palmer* (Marjorie Lord), *Ben* (Michael Winkelman), *Brady* (Andrew Duggan), *Palmer* (Richard Hale), *Susan* (Beverly Washburn), *Robinson* (Donald Randolph), *Lansing* (Kevin Hagen).

#2. The Jean LeBec Story
Written by: Dwight Newton & Boris Ingster
Directed by: Sidney Lanfield

Jean LeBec, a gifted violinist, agrees to escort Mary, the daughter of a once wealthy southern family who sponsored him, to California via the wagon train. To raise money, LeBec uses his violin as a stake in a card game. He wins, but is falsely accused of cheating and his violin is taken. When Mary attempts to buy the violin back, an argument ensues and LeBec is forced to kill the son of town owner Mark Hammond, in self defense. Flint McCullough, a witness, confirms this, yet Hammond refuses to provide the wagon train with provisions and supplies until Major Adams hands over Jean LeBec.

Jean (Ricardo Montalban), *Mary* (Joanna Moore), *Mark Hammond* (Grant Withers).

#3. The John Cameron Story

Written by: E. Jack Neuman
Directed by: George Waggner

On the wagon train headed west are John Cameron, a reserved ex-banker from Philadelphia, and his young, flirtatious wife Julie. When it appears that Julie has been abducted or run off with three brothers who joined the train for one night, John goes after them. Flint McCullough follows, knowing Cameron won't survive in the wilderness alone.

John Cameron (Michael Rennie), *Julie* (Carolyn Jones), *Charlie Otis* (Jack Elam), *Rich Hacker* (Claude Akins), *Frank Hacker* (William Boyett), *Paul Hacker* (Ted Mapes), *Trapper* (Francis McDonald).

#4. The Ruth Owens Story

Written by: Robert E. Thompson
Directed by: Robert Florey

Ruth Owens, a woman with a "checkered past," journeys west on the wagon train with her little girl and second husband, a teacher. Her brother Jimmy overtakes the train in an effort to find her. When a traveler makes insinuations about Ruth, a fight ensues and Jimmy kills the man. Then when Jimmy learns the man's remarks were true about Ruth, he refuses to defend himself.

Ruth Owens (Shelley Winters), *Jimmy Owens* (Dean Stockwell), *Paul* (Kent Smith).

#5. The Les Rand Story

Written by: Berne Giler
Directed by: Robert Florey

When Charlie Wooster is badly injured, the Major sends Flint to the nearest town to find a doctor. In the nearly deserted town of Little Fork, McCullough finds a few unfriendly people and learns the doctor is away. While he waits for his return, he meets Les Rand, a recent parolee. Rand holds the doctor (his father) responsible for his wife's death and plans to kill him.

Les Rand (Sterling Hayden), *Evie* (Sallie Brophy), *Dr. Rand* (Eduard Franz).

#6. The Nels Stack Story
Teleplay by: John Dunkel
Story by: Lester Dent
Director by: Don Weis

Nels Stack, a former Confederate officer, has become a pacifist. He is deeply resented by another southerner on the wagon train named Jeff Claymore who believes Stack is really a coward. When Native Americans raid the stock, a search party finds an old Indian man left to die. Stack refuses to leave the man behind and takes him along, which antagonizes Claymore and the others.

Nels Stack (Mark Stevens), *Laura Collins* (Joanne Dru), *Jeff Claymore* (Kevin Hagen), *Mrs. Hawks* (Irene Corlett), *Old Indian* (Charles Stevens).

#7. The Emily Rossiter Story
Teleplay by: Louis Peterson & Richard Collins
Story by: Boris Ingster
Directed by: Sidney Lanfield

When her husband is killed on the way to California, Emily Rossiter remarries to provide a home for her daughter. Her second husband is an overbearing stepfather and a ruthless bandit leader who robs the wagon train of a California land deed.

Emily Rossiter (Mercedes McCambridge), *Judy Rossiter* (Susan Oliver), *Ned Rossiter* (John Dehner), *Si* (Robert McQueeney), *Hank* (William Phipps).

#8. The John Darro Story
Written by: Adrian Spies
Directed by: Mark Stevens

John Darro travels on the train with his wife Aline and son Bobby. Darro was badly injured during the Civil War and walks with a limp.

Bobby worships his father and tells everyone he meets how proud he is of his Pa. Then Major Adams picks up an old man on the prairie who tells of a Native American massacre of a wagon train and a coward who refused to fight. According to the old man, the supposed coward was John Darro whom he knew by another name.

> *John Darro* (Eddie Albert), *Aline Darro* (Margo), *Bobby Darro* (Kim Charney), *Lucas* (Don Durant), *Old Man* (Edgar Buchanan).

#9. The Charles Avery Story
Written by: Aaron Spelling
Directed by: Bernard Girard

Major Adams and Flint McCullough encounter a small company of soldiers escorting Mokai, a Native American chief's daughter. She carries a peace treaty from Washington that will go into effect once she delivers it to her father. However, the group has been attacked by a renegade band, and Lieutenant Avery who is in charge has trouble keeping his men under control. Adams sends Flint along with them to ensure that the treaty gets safely to the chief.

Enroute Flint becomes aware of Avery's hostility toward Mokai and suspects that Avery's determination to reach the village involves more than the peace treaty.

> *Lieutenant Charles Avery* (Farley Granger), *Mokai* (Susan Kohner), *Private John Sumter* (Chuck Connors), *Private Cullen* (Bing Russell), *Running Horse* (Henry Brandon), *Big Bear* (Nico Minardos), *Choya* (Abel Fernandez), *Indian Brave* (Eddie Little Sky).

#10. The Mary Halstead Story
Teleplay by: Robert E. Thompson & Leo Lieberman
Story by: Leo Lieberman
Directed by: Justus Addiss

Mary Halstead is an elderly woman with a terminal illness. Her strongest wish is to find the son she abandoned as a child. She joins the train after receiving word from a lawyer who claims to know the whereabouts of her son. Enroute, Major Adams finds a young man left for dead on the trail with rope burns around his neck. While the travelers are suspicious, Mary forms an attachment to the young man who reminds her of her son. However, it appears someone tried to hang him and in his story lies the truth about Mary's son.

Mary Halstead (Agnes Moorehead), *Tracey* (Walter Coy), *Creegar* (Jack Lambert), *Tom* (Tom Pittman), *Laramie Kid* (Tom Laughlin), *Groton* (Gregg Palmer), *Ferguson* (Vaughn Taylor), *Kermit* (Robert Patten).

#11. The Zeke Thomas Story
Written by: Halsted Welles
Directed by: John Brahm

Flint McCullough and wagon train traveler Zeke Thomas search for a watering hole but find a hostile town instead. The Mayor and towns-people are intent on making the wagon train pay an unreasonable price for the use of their water. This sets up a confrontation between travelers and townsfolk. To complicate matters, the Mayor's mistress is Thomas's first wife whom he thought was dead.

Zeke Thomas (Gary Merill), *Maggie Thomas* (Janice Rule), *Violet* (K. T. Stevens).

#12. The Riley Gratton Story
Teleplay by: William Fay
Story by: Dwight Newton
Directed by: John Brahm

When con man Riley Gratton disappears after selling worthless land to the travelers, Adams pursues him, determined to get back the train members' money.

Riley (Guy Madison), *Sarah Dawson* (Karen Steele), *John Dawson* (Gregory Walcott), *McSorley* (James Westerfield), *Paul Dawson* (Greg Palmer), *Bixby* (Malcolm Atterbury).

#13. The Clara Beauchamp Story
Teleplay by: Winston Miller
Story by: William Leicester
Directed by: Earl Bellamy

Near a remote outpost on the western frontier, a new detachment of soldiers kill a Native American brave, unaware that their new commanding officer, Colonel Beauchamp has a territorial agreement with the local tribe. When the chief threatens to attack the train in retaliation, McCullough, with the Colonel, is able to arrange a social gathering between soldiers and tribesmen at the fort. Then Clara Beauchamp, the Colonel's alcoholic wife insults the chief, a potential peace agreement is ruined, and the wagon train is placed in jeopardy.

Clara Beauchamp (Nina Foch), *Col. Beauchamp* (Shepperd Strudwick), *Pearson* (Richard Garland), *Indian Chief* (Monte Blue), *Corporal* (Robert Swan), *Sergeant* (John Frederick), *Mrs. Hawks* (Irene Windust).

#14. The Julie Gage Story
Teleplay by: Aaron Spelling
Story by: Kermit Shelby
Directed by: Sidney Lanfield

Julie Gage is a very strong-willed, independent single woman traveling alone on the wagon train. Major Adams is concerned about her ability to cope. To help her, he recommends a number of men who prove incompatible. When one of them, Tobe Cannon, takes ill, Julie agrees to nurse him, when none of the other women on the train will, but faces the stigma of a single woman being alone with a single man.

Julie Gage (Anne Jeffreys), *Tobe Cannon* (Robert Sterling), *Jeff* (Don Megowan), *Buck* (James Komack), *Mrs. Hawks* (Irene Windust).

#15. The Cliff Grundy Story
Written by: Aaron Spelling
Directed by: George Waggner

Flint's old friend Cliff Grundy is severely injured hunting buffalo for the train, and can't be moved. The Major allows Flint to remain behind with another man to care for Grundy. However, that man is only interested in finding out the location of a gold mine Grundy planned to make claim to. Once he knows, he leaves McCullough and Grundy without food or water in hostile Indian territory.

Cliff Grundy (Dan Duryea), *Craig* (Russell Johnson), *The Man* (Don Durant), *Millard* (Harry Harvey, Jr.).

#16. The Luke O'Malley Story
Written by: William Fay
Directed by: Mark Stevens

A gambler, fleeing from a recently captured, notorious Mexican bandit, joins the wagon train posing as a parson. Major Adams eventually sees through his masquerade. Now the gambler tries in vain to convince people on the train that he is not a member of the outlaw gang.

Luke O'Malley (Keenan Wynn), *Martha* (Mary Murphy), *Dan* (Carlos Romero), *Katie* (Reba Waters).

#17. The Jesse Cowan Story
Written by: Dwight Newton
Directed by: Sidney Lanfield

Jesse Cowan, a Civil War veteran, rides after the wagon train to get revenge on the Beal family whom he holds responsible for the death of his family.

Jesse (George Montgomery), *Rufe Beal* (Lee Van Cleef), *Dorcas Beal* (Olive Carey), *Ansel Dale* (James Burke), *Bixby* (Malcolm Atterbury), *Bob Cowan* (Mort Mills), *Sally Jo Beal* (Penny Edwards), *Laura Beal* (Jeanne Bates).

#18. The Gabe Carswell Story
Written by: John Dunkel
Directed by: Earl Bellamy

Legendary scout Gabe Carswell has lived with the Arapaho Native Americans for many years. He has fathered a son, Little Elk, who has grown up with the Indian way of life and deeply resents the white man. When the wagon train crosses their territory, Little Elk wants to lead hostile tribesmen against them.

Gabe Carswell (James Whitmore), *Little Elk* (Scott Marlowe), *Running Bear* (Frank DeKova), *Chief Yellow Bear* (Thomas B. Henry).

#19. The Honorable Don Charlie Story
Teleplay by: Leo Townsend
Story by: Dwight Newton
Directed by: David Butler

Major Adams suspects trouble when an aging lothario focuses his attention on socialite Julie Wharton whom Adams has promised to escort safely to California.

Don Charlie (Caesar Romero), *Lottie Crane* (Virginia Grey), *Julie Wharton* (Diane Brewster), *Sgt. Muldey* (Hal Baylor), *Big Frank* (Ray Kellogg).

#20. The Dora Gray Story
Written by: E. Jack Neuman
Directed by: Arnold Laven

While investigating a Native American raid on a deserted farmhouse, Flint McCullough and Bill Hawks find evidence of gun running. McCullough decides to scout ahead and finds Doc Lockridge and Dora Gray camped with a wagon full of new army rifles.

Dora (Linda Darnell), *Doc* (John Carradine), *Lt. Miles Borden* (Mike Connors), *Sgt. Broderick* (Dan Blocker), *Colonel* (Tyler McVey), *Little Horse* (X Brands).

#21. The Annie MacGregor Story
Written by: Frank W. Marshall
Directed by: Mark Stevens

The MacGregors are a group of Scottish settlers headed west with kilts, bagpipes, and a strong sense of tradition. When Angus Mac-Gregor and his clan insist on their way of life, friction develops between them and the travelers. To add to the conflict, Annie MacGregor falls in love with Jason, a young American man on the train.

Annie (Jeannie Carson), *Angus* (Tudor Owen), *Jason* (Richard Long), *Claymore* (Kevin Hagen).

#22. The Bill Tawnee Story
Written by: Dwight Newton & Rik Vollaerts
Directed by: David Butler

Major Adams finds Bill Tawnee, a highly decorated Sioux scout who fought in the Civil War, on the trail with his wife and baby. When they join the train, the travelers are suspicious and fearful of Tawnee. When the major defends him, further problems arise.

Bill Tawnee (McDonald Carey), *George Barry* (Frank Cady), *Bixby* (Malcolm Atterbury), *Laverty* (Morgan Woodward), *Tucker* (William Fawcett).

#23. The Mark Hanford Story
Teleplay by: Turnley Walker & Emmett Roberts
Story by: Turnley Walker
Directed by: Jerry Hopper

Mark Hanford returns home from an eastern education to find his Native American mother dead, and his father, a wealthy rancher, about to wed a young bride from the wagon train. Bitter at his father's betrayal of his mother, Hanford embraces his Indian side and plans to take revenge.

Mark Hanford (Tom Tryon), *Jack Hanford* (Onslow Stevens), *Ann Jamison* (Kathleen Crowley), *Jake* (Paul Fix), *Martin* (I. Stanford Jolley).

#24. The Bernal Sierra Story
Teleplay by: Richard Maibaum
Story by: Gilbert Roland
Directed by: David Butler

Bernal Sierra, a follower of Juarez, joins Major Adam's wagon train to find two thieves who killed a guard and stole a cache of gold needed for Juarez's fight for freedom.

Sierra (Gilbert Roland), *Lorrie* (Dorothy Adams), *Casey* (Louis Jean Heydt), *Hughie* (Lane Bradford), *Art* (James Dobson).

#25. The Marie Dupree Story
Written by: Harry Brown
Directed by: Richard Bartlett

Vivacious and beautiful Marie Dupree causes trouble on the wagon train when she decides to play one man against the other to win her affections.

Marie Dupree (Debra Paget), *Tonio* (Nick Adams), *Bill Howard* (Robert Lowery), *Susie* (Dorothy Provine), *Joe* (Nicky Blair), *Dupree* (Raymond Greenleaf).

#26. A Man Called Horse
Teleplay by: Leo Townsend
Story by: Dorothy Johnson
Directed by: Sidney Lanfield

The wagon train comes upon a white man dressed as a Native American and caring for a sick and elderly Indian woman. Once they settle in, the man recounts a remarkable story of strength and courage.

Horse (Ralph Meeker), *Yellow Robe* (Michael Pate), *Mother* (Celia Lovsky), *Bright Star* (Joan Taylor), *Lucinda* (Jorie Wyler).

#27. The Sally Drummond Story
Teleplay by: Norman Jolley & Richart Bartlett
Story by: Lester William Berke
Directed by: Richard Bartlett

Flint McCullough takes shelter from the storm with Sarah and Jeb Drummond and finds the couple involved in a bitter relationship. To repay their hospitality, Flint makes an effort to bring them together.

Sarah (June Lockhart), *Jeb Drummond* (Gene Evans), *Walt Archer* (William Talman), *Molly Archer* (Debbie Hengen).

#28. The Sally Potter Story
Written by: Doris & Frank Hursley
Directed by: David Butler

Sally Potter joins the wagon train and causes a reaction among the men. Joe Trumbell and his nephew Matt are both enamored of Sally. But as both fall in love with her, their own relationship becomes venomous.

Sally Potter (Vanessa Brown), *Matt Trumbell* (Martin Milner), *Joe Trumbell* (Lyle Bettger), *Henry Bennett* (King Donovan), *Millie Bennett* (Jocelyn Brando), *Billings* (Brad Dexter), *Jimmy Bennett* (Johnny Crawford).

#29. The Daniel Barrister Story
Teleplay by: Norman Jolley
Story by: Norman Jolley & Richard Bartlett
Directed by: Richard Bartlett

When Daniel Barrister's wife is seriously injured in an accident, Daniel rejects all medical treatment and places his faith in the Lord. When infection sets in, Major Adams overrules him and sends Flint for a doctor in a nearby town. When Flint arrives he finds the entire town quarantined due to an outbreak of smallpox.

Daniel Barrister (Charles Bickford), *Dr. Peter Culver* (Roger Smith), *Mr. Miller* (Alan Lane), *Mrs. Snyder* (Sarah Selby), *Guard* (Arthur Space).

#30. The Major Adams Story *(Part One)*
Written by: Frank W. Marshall
Directed by: Mark Stevens

A look back at Major Seth Adams' life at the outbreak of the Civil War, his ill-fated romance with Ranie Webster, being wounded in the war, and his growing friendship with Charlie Wooster and Bill Hawks.

Ranie Webster (Virginia Grey), *Mrs. Hawks* (Irene Windust), *Colonel Hillary* (Douglas Kennedy), *Mary Bradley* (Kay Stewart).

#31. The Major Adams Story *(Part Two)*
Written by: Frank W. Marshall
Directed by: Mark Stevens

After the war, Seth Adams retires from the U.S. Army. Upon learning that Ranie Webster married someone else during the war, Adams decides to become a wagonmaster, guiding trains from Missouri to California.

On the wagon trip west years later, he once again encounters Ranie, now a widow. Adams is eager to begin his life again with Ranie, but she seems reluctant. Competing with Adams for Ranie's hand is Colonel Hillary, an ex-Confederate officer, and a relentless suitor who won't take no for an answer.

Ranie Webster (Virginia Grey), *Colonel Hillary* (Douglas Kennedy).

#32. The Charles Maury Story
Written by: Robert Yale Libott
Directed by: Allen Miner

The Major and Flint are concerned about a possible attack from Maury's Marauders, a band of renegade Confederates who prey on unprotected wagon trains. When a group of Union soldiers offer to accompany the wagon, Adams gladly accepts, but he soon becomes suspicious of their intentions. The leader seems too friendly with a woman passenger who dislikes Yankees.

Juliette Creston (Wanda Hendrix), *Charles Maury* (Charles Drake), *Matt Goslett* (House Peters, Jr.), *Luke Goslett* (George Keymas), *Tom Rainey* (Steve Rowland).

#33. The Dan Hogan Story
Written by: William Fay
Directed by: Richard Bartlett

In the small town of Sweet Sabbath, Major Adams recognizes Dan Hogan, a fighter he once managed. Hogan has turned down the job of deputy sheriff because he refuses to carry a gun. Then Dan comes up against the town bully who threatens his life.

Dan Hogan (Jock Mahoney), *Hyman Ranse* (John Larch), *Mary Hogan* (Rachel Ames), *Marshall* (Tom Greenway), *George* (Richard Cutting), *Cliff Shields* (Simon Scott).

#34. The Ruttledge Munroe Story
Teleplay by: Norman Jolley
Story by: Norman Jolley & Richard Bartlett
Directed by: Richard Bartlett

Major Adams admits a young drifter named Ruttledge Munroe who claims to have lost his horse. After Munroe shoots and kills two men trying to rob the wagon train, he offers to protect Ruth Hadley and her baby. Ruth fears Munroe who in reality is a cold-blooded killer out to seek revenge on the Major for a wartime incident.

Ruttledge Munroe (John Barrymore, Jr.), *Ruth Hadley* (Mala Powers), *Masters* (William Tannen), *Mrs. Mitchell* (Helen Brown), *Mr. Mitchell* (George Eldredge).

#35. The Rex Montana Story
Written by: Warren Wilson
Directed by: Jesse Hibbs

Rex Montana and his Wild West Show join the wagon train. Rex's reputation for adventure and bravery are almost legendary, but Seth Adams and Flint McCullough begin to doubt Montana is all he's supposed to be.

Rex Montana (Forrest Tucker), *Clyde Winslow* (James Dunn), *Loetha* (Kristine Miller), *Rodney Miller* (Peter Whitney), *Bill* (Myron Healey), *Shanwaukee* (Joseph Vitale).

#36. The Cassie Tanner Story
Written by: Paul Savage
Directed by: Mark Stevens

Flint McCullough rescues Cassie Tanner, a rough, outspoken woman, from an Indian attack, then invites her to join the train. When Cassie meets Major Adams, she makes up her mind that he is the man for her.

Cassie Tanner (Marjorie Main), *Clee McMasters* (George Chandler).

#37. The John Wilbot Story
Written by: Richard Maibaum
Directed by: Mark Stevens

When Adams and McCullough argue about who works harder, they switch jobs temporarily to settle the argument. Then Flint winds up in the middle of a heated argument when an abolitionist accuses a school teacher with a limp of being John Wilkes Booth.

John Wilbot (Dane Clark), *Roy Pelham* (Robert Vaughn), *Harriet Field* (Audrey Dalton), *Thaddeus Field* (Tyler McVey), *Arthur Pelham* (Orville Sherman), *Broxton* (Roy Engel).

#38. The Monty Britton Story
Written by: Thomas Thompson
Directed by: Mark Stevens

Major Adams sends Flint out to locate water. The train supply is running dangerously low. When Flint doesn't return, Adams goes looking and finds him delirious and the waterhole poisoned. Their last hope is Fort Paiute, but the only man who knows where the fort is refuses to help.

Monty Britton (Ray Danton), *Garth Redmond* (Claude Akins), *Betty Britton* (Mona Freeman), *Rev. Sumpter* (John Hoyt).

#39. The Sacramento Story
Written by: Thomas Thompson
Directed by: Richard Bartlett

The wagon train finally arrives in Sacramento, California. Maxwell Revere and his daughter Julie are eager to see the ranch he bought sight unseen. In an effort to help them, Flint discovers it's a swamp. Instead he leads them to an area of fertile land, then goes after the swindler.

Cliff Gundy (Dan Duryea), *Dora Gray* (Linda Darnell), *Cassie Tanner* (Marjorie Main), Julie Revere (Margaret O'Brien), *Clee McMasters* (George Chandler), *Mort Galvin* (Reed Hadley), *Maxwell Revere* (Harry Stevens).

WAGON TRAIN
Season Two: 1958-1959

Episode Titles	Air Dates
40. Around the Horn	10/1/58
41. The Juan Ortega Story	10/8/58
42. The Jennifer Churchill Story	10/15/58
43. The Tobias Jones Story	10/22/58
44. The Liam Fitzmorgan Story	10/29/58
45. The Doctor Willoughby Story	1/5/58
46. The Bije Wilcox Story	11/19/58
47. The Millie Davis Story	11/26/58
48. The Sakae Ito Story	12/3/58
49. The Tent City Story	12/10/58
50. The Beauty Jamison Story	12/17/58
51. The Mary Ellen Thomas Story	12/24/58
52. The Dick Richardson Story	12/31/58
53. The Kitty Angel Story	1/7/59
54. The Flint McCullough Story	1/14/59
55. The Hunter Malloy Story	1/21/59
56. The Ben Courtney Story	1/28/59
57. The Ella Lindstrom Story	2/4/59
58. The Last Man	2/11/59
59. The Old Man Charvanaugh Story	2/18/59
60. The Annie Griffith Story	2/25/59
61. The Jasper Cato Story	3/4/59
62. The Vivian Carter Story	3/11/59
63. The Conchita Vasquez Story	3/18/59
64. The Sister Rita Story	3/25/59

Episode Titles	*Air Dates*
65. The Matthew Lowry Story	4/1/59
66. The Swift Cloud Story	4/8/59
67. The Vincent Eaglewood Story	4/15/59
68. The Clara Duncan Story	4/22/59
69. The Duke Lemay Story	4/29/59
70. The Kate Parker Story	5/6/59
71. The Steve Campden Story	5/13/59
72. Chuck Wooster, Wagonmaster	5/20/59
73. The Jose Maria Moran Story	5/27/59
74. The Andrew Hale Story	6/3/59
75. The Rodney Lawrence Story	6/10/59
76. The Steele Family	6/17/59
77. The Jenny Tannen Story	6/24/59

#40. Around The Horn
Written by: Ted Sherdeman
Directed by: Herschel Daugherty

While in San Francisco Major Adams, Hawks and Wooster are shang-haied aboard a schooner headed for New Orleans by way of South America.

Willy Moran (Ernest Borgnine), *Captain Cobb* (William Bendix), *Ferris* (Marc Lawrence), *Freddy* (Gil Perkins).

#41. The Juan Ortega Story
Teleplay by: David Swift, & Peggy and Lou Shaw
Story by: Frank Waldman
Directed by: David Swift

Seth Adams and Flint McCullough find Juan Ortega in shock after witnessing his father lynched by three men. They take Ortega back to the train and enroute find a man who has been tortured by Indians and near death. Ortega's knowledge of native herbs helps to heal the man. Then Adams discovers the man is one of the three men that hung Ortega's father.

Juan Ortega (Dean Stockwell), *Jay Thorton* (Robert F. Simon), *Tuck Edwards* (Vic Perrin), *Jarvis* (Robert Osterloh), *Father Martin* (Paul Langton).

#42. The Jennifer Churchill Story
Written by: Robert Yale Libott
Directed by: Jerry Hopper

Jennifer Churchill runs away from her father and an arranged mar-riage. She joins the wagon train. Flint discovers her father has offered a large reward for her return, so he tries to help her escape, knowing she'll be prey to bounty hunters.

Jennifer Churchill (Rhonda Fleming), *Fred* (Andy Clyde), *Mr. Churchill* (Paul Maxey), *Ned* (Eddy Waller).

#43. The Tobias Jones Story
Written by: Harry Von Zell
Directed by: Herschel Daugherty

Midge, a young orphan, attaches herself to a homeless drifter named Tobias Jones. Together they stow away on the wagon train. When Adams discovers them, he puts them to work to earn their keep. The travelers are distrustful of Tobias, then one of the passengers is found murdered with his knife.

Tobias Jones (Lou Costello), *Midge* (Beverly Washburn), *Nathaniel Ferguson* (Harry Von Zell), *Michael Folsom* (Morris Ankrum), *Alf Meadows* (Peter Breck), *Martha* (June Clayworth).

#44. The Liam Fitzmorgan Story
Written by: Robert E. Thompson
Directed by: Herschel Daugherty

Irish freedom fighter Liam Fitzmorgan has been ordered to find a traitor responsible for the death of several of their members. When he finds out the man he's after is on the wagon train, he joins up to find him.

Liam Fitzmorgan (Cliff Robertson), *Laura Grady* (Audrey Dalton), *James Grady* (Rhys Williams), *Carney* (Terence de Marney), *Michael Dermoth* (David Leland).

#45. The Doctor Willoughby Story
Written by: Harry Von Zell
Directed by: Allen Miner

Dr. Carol Willoughby is headed west to practice medicine. Enroute, a severely injured Native American chief is brought to her with an ultimatum: save him or his tribe will attack the train.

Dr. Carol Willoughby (Jane Wyman), *Hank Simmons* (Orville Sherman), *Bart Grover* (Alan Marshall), *Mrs. Parker* (Ethel Shutta).

#46. The Bije Wilcox Story
Written by: Milton Krims
Directed by: Abner Biberman

Francis Mason joins the wagon train to find his missing brother. He tells Major Adams that a man named Bije Wilcox has written him, telling him that he has information as to his brother's whereabouts. Mason is to meet him in California.

Bije Wilcox (Chill Wills), *Mason* (Onslow Stevens), *Medicine Mark* (Lawrence Dobkin), *Bull Man* (Abraham Sofaer), *1st Son* (Richard Evans).

#47. The Millie Davis Story
Written by: Leo Townsend
Directed by: Jerry Hopper

In a town ahead of the train, McCullough meets old friend Millie Davis and her adopted daughter Penny whom she's raised from infancy. When a woman arrives who claims to be Penny's grand-mother, Millie fears losing custody of Penny, so she tells the woman that she and McCullough are the parents of the child.

Millie Davis (Nancy Gates), *Penny* (Evelyn Rudie), *Mrs. Winston* (Eleanor Audley), *Albert Sykes* (Whit Bissell), *Pete Bailey* (Irving Bacon), *Judd* (Chubby Johnson), *Martha* (Amzie Strickland), *Ike* (James Coburn).

#48. The Sakae Ito Story
Written by: Gene L. Coon
Directed by: Herschel Daugherty

Along the trail, Seth Adams finds two Japanese: a Samurai Warrior and his servant. They are enroute to California and carry a large urn. Three men suspect that the urn contains gold, so they steal it and run away.

Sakae Ito (Sessue Hayakawa), *Matsu* (Robert Kino), *Sailor Blaine* (James Griffith), *Tom Revere* (Jack Lambert), *Burt Rake* (Dennis Moore), *Burl Miching* (Henry Rowland).

#49. The Tent City Story
Written by: Norman Jolley
Directed by: Richard Bartlett

Flint McCullough disapproves of Major Adams' punishment of a wagon train member who shot a buffalo on Indian hunting grounds. When the man is placed in chains, an argument ensues and Flint leaves the train. He then becomes the Marshal of Tent City.

Will Hardesty (Wayne Morris), *Goldie* (Audrey Totter), *Rafe* (Slim Pickens), *White Eagle* (Peter Coe), *Mrs. Parker* (Yvonne White), *Bartender* (Earl Hansen).

#50. The Beauty Jamison Story
Written by: Frank Moss
Directed by: Richard Bartlett

Ranch Owner Beauty Jamison controls the largest amount of land in the territory and seeks to wrest land from the surrounding smaller ranchers as well. She refuses to allow McCullough and the wagon train to cross her land, claiming he sides with the smaller ranchers opposing her.

Beauty (Virginia Mayo), *Steve Marshall* (Russell Johnson), *Ken Mayer* (Bascombe), *Grimes* (Frank Gerstle), *Luke Carter* (Phil Chambers), *Ralph Jessup* (Charles Tannen).

#51. The Mary Ellen Thomas Story
Teleplay by: Gene L. Coon & Harry Junkin
Story by: James A. Parker & Howard Christie
Directed by: Virgil Vogel

Sally Mayhew, a girl with a terminal illness, makes friends with Mary Ellen Thomas, another girl on the train who has alienated herself from the travelers with an unhappy disposition.

Mary Ellen (Patricia McCormack), *Sally* (Jenny Hecht), *Ben Mayhew* (Richard Cutting), *Mrs. Mayhew* (Claudia Bryar).

#52. The Dick Richardson Story
Written by: Gene L. Coon, Martin Berkeley & Clark Reynolds
Directed by: David Butler

Major Adams entrusts Dick Richardson with money from the train's emergency fund to buy replacement horses in the next town. Then his companion's riderless horse returns to the train.

Dick Richardson (John Ericson), *Molly Richardson* (Betty Lynn), *Laura Milford* (Aline Towne), *Ken Milford* (Lyle Talbot), *Erna Logan* (Jeanne Bates).

#53. The Kitty Angel Story
Written by: Leonard Praskins
Directed by: James Neilson

Kitty Angel, a woman with a questionable past, is rejected by the other women on the wagon train. Kitty is also the only woman to show compassion for an orphaned Native American baby. When the infant contracts smallpox, members of the train fear an epidemic and pressure Major Adams to leave Kitty and the baby behind.

Kitty Angel (Anne Baxter), *Obediah Finch* (Henry Hull), *Cassie Holden* (Vivi Janiss), *Sairy Hogg* (Kathleen Freeman), *Sam Hogg* (David Leland), *Indian Brave* (Abel Fernandez).

#54. The Flint McCullough Story
Teleplay by: Harry Von Zell
Story by: E. Jack Neuman
Directed by: Allen Miner

Flint McCullough arrives at Fort Bridger where he once was based, and finds Jase Taylor, a former Confederate Colonel he once swore he'd kill.

Jim Bridger (Theodore Newton), *Col. Jase Taylor* (Everett Sloane), *Jean Yates* (Rebecca Welles). *Tom Yates* (Milton Frome), *Lt. Abbott* (Charles Cooper).

#55. The Hunter Malloy Story
Teleplay by: Thomas Thompson & Gene L. Coon
Story by: Thomas Thompson
Directed by: Allen Miner

Hunter Malloy and his partner plan to rob a young married couple of their life savings, but discover gold along the trail before they commit the robbery. Meanwhile, Major Adams warns his travelers of impending snow storms and cautions them to move on, yet no one takes his warning seriously.

Malloy (Lloyd Nolan), *Ted Garner* (Troy Donahue), *Natalie Garner* (Luanna Patten), *Whitey Burke* (Terence de Marney), *Clegg* (Bill Erwin), *Radford* (Joe Abdullah).

#56. The Ben Courtney Story
Written by: Gene L. Coon & Rik Vollaerts
Directed by: Abner Biberman

Flint McCullough escorts two families from the wagon train to Bitter Springs. One family includes two adopted children, one of them a young Afro-American boy named Daniel. However, when they reach the town, the sheriff refuses to let them join the settlement unless they give up Daniel.

Ben Courtney (Stephen McNally), *John Ramsey* (John Larch), *Nora Courtney* (Rachel Ames), *Michael* (Roger Mobley), *Mayor Storey* (Arthur Space), *Daniel* (Darryl Glenn), *Rev. Butler* (Richard Hale), *Leona Ramsey* (Kay Stewart).

#57. The Ella Lindstrom Story
Written and Directed by: Allen Miner

On the journey west, Ella Lindstrom's husband dies, leaving her to care for their seven children, one of them physically challenged.

Ella Lindstrom (Betty Davis), *Fitzpatrick* (Robert Fuller), *Dr. Monroe* (Alex Gerry), *Inga* (Cindy Robbins), *Stig* (Harold Daye), *Britt* (Susan Henning), *Bo* (Bobby Buntrock).

#58. The Last Man
Teleplay by: Larry Marcus
Story by: James Gunn
Directed by: James Neilson

Flint McCullough finds a disheveled man along the trail in need of attention. Later Major Adams and McCullough find a diary among debris of an early wagon train that indicates the stranger's survival cost the lives of the other travelers. Once other members of the train find out, they demand justice.

Stranger (Dan Duryea), *Ellen Emerson* (Judi Meredith), *Mr. Emerson* (Damian O'Flynn), *Mr. Wentworth* (Wilton Graff), *Harris* (Marx Hartman)

#59. The Old Man Charvanaugh Story
Written by: Arthur Browne, Jr.
Directed by: Virgil Vogel

Old man Charvanaugh, a heartless bandit, poses as a concertina-playing wanderer, then robs Flint McCullough and a family he's escorting to a settlement. As a result, Flint and party are left without needed supplies and clothing.

Charvanaugh (J. Carrol Naish). *Helen Lerner* (Dorothy Green), *Squirrel Charvanaugh* (L. Q. Jones), *Sybil Lerner* (Bernadette Withers), *Duane Lerner* (Ricky Klein), *Tucknis* (Jeff Daley), *Josh* (Quintin Sondergaard).

#60. The Annie Griffith Story
Written by: Kathleen Hite
Directed by: Jerry Hopper

Flint McCullough is ambushed by Native Americans and badly wounded while searching for a pass in the snow-covered mountains. A rugged, unkempt woman finds him and nurses him back to health. Once Flint is well enough, the woman intends to give him to the Native Americans, hoping that in return, they will get her back to civilization.

Annie Griffith (Jan Sterling), *Cleve Colter* (John Dehner), *Blade Griffith* (Robert Anderson), *Old Man* (Clem Bevans).

#61. The Jasper Cato Story
Teleplay by: Robert Yale Libott & Frank Phares
Story by: Frank Phares
Directed by: Arthur Hiller

Bostonian Jasper Cato joins the wagon train, anxious to find Jim Collins, a small-town newspaper editor and friend of Major Adams. The Major becomes suspicious and tries to reach Collins before Cato does.

Jasper Cato (Brian Donlevy), *Jim Collins* (Allen Case).

#62. The Vivian Carter Story
Written by: Peggy & Lou Shaw
Directed by: Joseph Pevney

Vivian Carter travels with the train to meet her fiancé in a small western town. Enroute, a fellow traveler falls in love with her.

Vivian Carter (Phyllis Thaxter), *Bert Carter* (Patric Knowles), *Christopher Webb* (Lorne Greene), *Mrs. Anderson* (Jane Darwell).

#63. The Conchita Vasquez Story
Teleplay by: Thelma Schnee
Story by: Aaron Spelling
Directed by: Jerry Hopper

Conchita Vasquez, a pretty Spanish-Native American woman, lures Flint into a trap so that her people can capture and hold him for ransom. Then after his capture, Conchita decides to help him escape.

Conchita (Anna Maria Alberghetti), *Carlos Soldareo* (Carlos Romero), *Martha Williams* (Joyce Meadows), *Wes Arthur* (John Goddard), *Simon Williams* (Alan Reynolds), *Dan Jaeger* (William Lundmark).

#64. The Sister Rita Story
Written by: Gerry Day
Directed by: Joseph Pevney

Flint aids three nuns on their way to Nevada to start a Native American Mission school. Although their ways are foreign to him, Flint and the nuns develop a rapport and he finds himself particularly drawn to Sister Rita.

Sister Rita (Vera Miles), *Sister Joseph* (Frances Bavier), *Sister Monica* (Sylvia Marriott), *Juan* (Lalo Rios).

#65. The Mathew Lowry Story
Teleplay by: Leonard Praskins
Story by: Paul David
Directed by: Jack Arnold

Traveler Jed Otis constantly ridicules Mathew Lowry, a Quaker, who has lost an arm. Lowry's younger brother believes he's a coward despite his pacifist beliefs.

Mathew Lowry (Richard Anderson), *Rebecca* (Cathleen Nesbitt), *Jed Otis* (John Pickard), *Benjamin* (Ronald Anton), *Lane* (Pat Brady).

#66. The Swift Cloud Story
Written by: Donald S. Sanford
Directed by: Virgil Vogel

Major Adams captures Swift Cloud, the crippled son of a Native American chief, during a raid on the wagons. When it's discovered that Swift Cloud's condition can be cured, Adams barters for the wagon train's safety.

Swift Cloud (Rafael Campos), *Tommy Peeks* (Johnny Washbrook), *Fire Cloud* (Henry Brandon), *Jed Harcourt* (Alan Baxter).

#67. The Vincent Eaglewood Story
Written by: David Swift
Directed by: Jerry Hopper

Vincent Eaglewood is hired to be the school teacher for the children on the wagon train. However, Eaglewood takes his job so seriously that it begins to concern Major Adams.

> *Vincent* (Wally Cox), *Erika Hennepin* (Gail Kobe), *Ben Denike* (Read Morgan), *Bryngelson* (Guinn Williams), *Oma Jean* (Karen Sue Trent), *Elwood Hennepin* (Robert Eyer).

#68. The Clara Duncan Story
Written by: Richard Collins & Warren Wilson
Directed by: Jerry Hopper

Clara Duncan and her future father-in-law head west to find fiancé-artist Claude Soriano. Then McCullough and a newspaperman find a painting by Soriano which leads them to believe the artist's life is in jeopardy.

> *Clara Duncan* (Angie Dickinson), *Sylvio Soriano* (Eduardo Ciannelli), *Roger Garrett* (William Reynolds), *Claude Soriano* (Robert Clarke), *Steve Wilson* (Myron Healey).

#69. The Duke LeMay Story
Teleplay by: Robert Fresco
Story by: Virgil Vogel & Robert Fresco
Directed by: Virgil Vogel

Duke LeMay, an escaped convict joins the wagon train to escape from justice. When a sheriff arrives, LeMay becomes frightened, shoots him and flees.

> *Duke* (Cameron Mitchell), *Sarah* (Joan Evans), *Matthew Sinclair* (Edward Platt), *Davey* (Terry Kelman).

#70. The Kate Parker Story
Written by: Leonard Praskins
Directed by: Tay Garnett

When Evie Finley is injured while traveling, Kate Parker offers to remain behind with Evie and her husband while the train rolls on to the next town for a doctor. Once the train leaves, Kate's husband Jonas decides to kill the Finleys and steal the gold that they've been carrying.

Kate Parker (Virginia Grey), *Jonas Parker* (Warren Stevens), *Chris Finley* (Robert Fuller), *Evie Finley* (Ruta Lee), *Boone Caulder* (Royal Dano).

#71. The Steve Campden Story
Written by: Robert Yale Libott
Directed by: Christian Nyby

A snowstorm blocks the advance of the wagon train. Flint McCullough, Steve Campden and his son search for a mountain pass, but are forced to seek refuge in a cave.

Steve Campden (Torin Thatcher), *Steve* (Ben Cooper).

#72. Chuck Wooster, Wagonmaster
Written by: Nat Tanchuck & Arthur Browne, Jr.
Directed by: Virgil Vogel

During a blizzard, the wagon train is stopped at a mountain pass. Flint is sent to scout what's ahead but never returns. When Major Adams and Bill Hawks ride off to look for him, they too disappear without a trace. Now Charlie Wooster is left to run things and get the train to another pass further south before everyone panics.

Wilkins (Harry Carey, Jr.), *John Loring* (Douglas Kennedy), *Sarah Duncan* (Jean Inness).

#73. The Jose Maria Moran Story
Written by: Paul King & Joe Stone
Directed by: Tay Garnett

The wagons come upon a man staked out and left to die by the Shoshone Indians. Major Adams learns that he is Jose Maria Moran, a Spanish-Irish renegade who has lived with the Pawnees for years. When the Shoshones learn that Moran has been saved, they threaten to attack the train unless he is returned to them.

Jose Maria Moran (Robert Loggia), *Mary Naughton* (Audrey Dalton), *Tim Naughton* (Tudor Owen), *Don Luis Salazar* (Anthony Caruso).

#74. The Andrew Hale Story
Teleplay by: Jean Holloway & Peter Barry
Story by: Peter Barry
Directed by: Virgil Vogel

Preacher Andrew Hale kills one of his parishioners in a shooting accident. Dazed by the incident, Hale strays off into the desert where he encounters the wagon train.

Andrew Hale (John McIntire), *Garth English* (James Best), *Martha English* (Louise Fletcher), *Mrs. Anderson* (Jane Darwell), *Joe Hamplar* (Jack Buetel), *Elliot Garrison* (Clu Gulager).

#75. The Rodney Lawrence Story
Written by: Gerry Day
Directed by: Virgil Vogel

The wagon train encounters a group of wandering Native Americans, among whom is a young white man they have raised from childhood. Ocheo, the boy's foster father, sees the opportunity for the young man to return to his own way of life and urges him to join the train.

Rodney Lawrence (Dean Stockwell), *Ocheo* (Frank DeKova), *Mindy McCrea* (Cindy Robbins).

#76. The Steele Family
Written by: Jean Holloway
Directed by: Christian Nyby

The mother of four eligible daughters joins the train and seeks Major Adams' aid in finding some likely prospects.

Mrs. Steele (Lee Patrick), *Charity* (Lori Nelson), *Faith* (Barbara Eiler), *Prudence* (Diane Jergens), *Hope* (Penny Edwards).

#77. The Jenny Tannen Story
Teleplay by: Kathleen Hite
Story by: Howard Christie & James A. Parker
Directed by: Christian Nyby

Phoebe Tannen joins the wagon train to travel to San Francisco and locate her mother. Enroute, Phoebe is blinded in an accident. Major Adams promises to help her find her mother upon their arrival.

Jenny/Phoebe Tannen (Ann Blyth), *John Barclay* (Chuck Henderson), *Rollie Malvin* (William Hunt), *Mrs. Malvin* (Jean Harvey), *Doctor* (Howard Wright).

WAGON TRAIN
Season Three: 1959-1960

Episode Titles	Air Dates
78. The Stagecoach Story	9/30/59
79. The Greenhorn Story	10/7/59
80. The C. L. Harding Story	10/14/59
81. The Estaban Zamora Story	10/21/59
82. The Elizabeth McQueeny Story	10/28/59
83. The Martha Barham Story	11/4/59
84. The Cappy Darrin Story	11/11/59
85. The Felizia Kingdom Story	11/18/59
86. The Jess MacAbbee Story	11/25/59
87. The Danny Benedict Story	12/2/59
88. The Vittorio Bottecelli Story	12/16/59
89. The St. Nicholas Story	12/23/59
90. The Ruth Marshall Story	12/30/59
91. The Lita Foladaire Story	1/6/60
92. The Colonel Harris Story	1/13/60
93. The Marie Brant Story	1/20/60
94. The Larry Hanify Story	1/27/60
95. The Clayton Tucker Story	2/10/60
96. The Benjamin Burns Story	2/17/60
97. The Ricky and Laurie Bell Story	2/24/60
98. The Tom Tuckett Story	3/2/60
99. The Tracy Sadler Story	3/9/60
100. The Alexander Portlass Story	3/16/60
101. The Christine Elliot Story	3/23/60
102. The Joshua Gilliam Story	3/30/60

Episode Titles	Air Dates
103. The Maggie Hamilton Story	4/6/60
104. The Jonas Murdock Story	4/13/60
105. The Amos Gibbon Story	4/20/60
106. Trial for Murder *(Part One)*	4/27/60
107. Trial for Murder *(Part Two)*	5/4/60
108. The Countess Baranof Story	5/11/60
109. The Dick Jarvis Story	5/18/60
110. The Dr. Swift Cloud Story	5/25/60
111. The Luke Grant Story	6/1/60
112. The Charlene Brenton Story	6/8/60
113. The Sam Livingston Story	6/15/60
114. The Shad Bennington Story	6/22/60

#78. The Stagecoach Story
Written by: Jean Holloway
Directed by: William Witney

After an enjoyable time in San Francisco, Adams, Hawks, and Wooster buy stagecoach tickets to return to St. Louis, Missouri. They soon discover their driver is none other than Flint McCullough, and the trip proves to be quite an adventure.

Angela DeVarga (Debra Paget), *Caleb Jamison* (Clu Gulager), *Benito DeVarga* (Henry Darrow), *Antonio* (Abraham Sofaer).

#79. The Greenhorn Story
Written by: Jean Holloway
Directed by: Bretaigne Windust

Samuel T. Evans, a young easterner, joins the wagon train. Major Adams is amused by his obvious naiveté, but later becomes concerned at the problems Evans causes.

Samuel T. Evans (Mickey Rooney), *Aunt Em* (Ellen Corby), *Humphrey Pumpret* (Byron Foulger), *Melanie Pumpret* (Daria Massey).

#80. The C. L. Harding Story
Teleplay by: Jean Holloway
Story by: Howard Christie & Jean Holloway
Directed by: Herschel Daugherty

A woman newspaper reporter is assigned to travel with the wagon train. Once aboard, she begins a woman's suffrage movement among the wives.

C. L. Harding (Claire Trevor), *Arietta* (Amzie Strickland), *Buzz* (Theodore Newton), *Estrabella* (Jean Ingram).

#81. The Estaban Zamora Story

Written by: Halsey Melone
Directed by: Bretaigne Windust

Immigrant Estaban Zamora joins the wagon train to meet his three sons working for a sheep farmer. Upon arrival, he discovers his youngest son was killed and he vows revenge.

Estaban (Ernest Borgnine), *Bernabe Zamora* (Leonard Nimoy), *Manuel* (Phillip Pine), *Roy Daniels* (Robert Armstrong), *Sheriff Hixon* (Stuart Randall).

#82. The Elizabeth McQueeny Story

Written & Directed by: Allen Miner

Elizabeth McQueeny joins Major Adams' wagon train with a group of lovely young women. She informs the travelers she is taking the girls west to start a finishing school. The train members are suspicious and distrustful.

Elizabeth (Bette Davis), *Roxanne* (Maggie Pierce), *Count* (Robert Strauss), *Phil* (Barney Biro).

#83. The Martha Barham Story

Teleplay by: Dale and Katherine Eunson
Story by: Howard Christie & James A. Parker
Directed by: James Neilson

Flint McCullough arrives at an army post with a Sioux companion, and is accused by the post commander's daughter of being a renegade. Then the girl's fiancé is captured by Native Americans and she asks McCullough to help rescue him.

Martha Barham (Ann Blyth), *Major Barham* (Dayton Lummis), *Curly Horse* (Read Morgan), *Silas* (Warren Oates), *Black Panther* (Henry Brandon).

#84. The Cappy Darrin Story
Written by: Stanley Kallis
Directed by: Virgil Vogel

Cappy Darrin, an older riverboat captain, joins the train with grandson Tuck. Near their destination, he and the boy decide to leave the train and journey on their own to California.

Cappy Darrin (Ed Wynn), *Tuck* (Tom Nolan), *Mason Hardy* (Tyler McVey).

#85. The Felizia Kingdom Story
Written by: Sloan Nibley & Leonard Praskins
Directed by: Joseph Pevney

Flint McCullough rides to the ranch of Felizia Kingdom to ask for permission for the wagon train to cross her land, and is taken captive by the strong-willed woman.

Felizia Kingdom (Judith Anderson), *Snare* (Larry Peron), *Angela* (Jean Allison).

#86. The Jess MacAbbee Story
Teleplay by: Jean Holloway
Story by: Howard Christie & James A. Parker
Directed by: David Butler

Flint McCullough comes upon the ranch of Jess MacAbbee who appears to be hiding something. The scout discovers that MacAbbee has five beautiful daughters that he doesn't want McCullough to know about.

Jess (Andy Devine), *Bell MacAbbee* (Glenda Farrell), *Lilly Belle* (Carol Byron), *Anna Belle* (Karen Green), *Cora Belle* (Tammy Marihugh), *Jed Culpepper* (Ray Teal).

#87. The Danny Benedict Story
Written by: Harold Swanton
Directed by: Herschel Daugherty

Danny Benedict is unhappy with the strict military life of his father, and runs away when his father threatens to punish him in public.

Danny (Brandon DeWilde), *Colonel Benedict* (Onslow Stevens), *Harrison* (Walter Reed), *Prissy* (Melinda Plowman).

#88. The Vittorio Bottecelli Story
Teleplay by: Jean Holloway
Story by: Jean Holloway & Howard Christie
Directed by: Jerry Hopper

Italian Duke Vittorio Bottecelli attempts to charm some married women on the wagon train, and Major Adams warns him to stop before some angry husbands react.

Bottecelli (Gustavo Rojo), *Julie Carson* (Elizabeth Montgomery), *Tod* (James Lydon), *Josef* (Anthony Caruso), *Count* (Edgar Barrier).

#89. The St. Nicholas Story
Written by: Jean Holloway
Directed by: Bretaigne Windust

The wagon train stops to make camp on Christmas Eve, and young Jimmy Sherman wanders away and meets Little Eagle, a Native American youth.

Jimmy (Johnny Bangert), *Little Eagle* (Edward Vargas), *Papa Kling* (Robert Emhardt), *Mama Kling* (Elizabeth Fraser).

#90. The Ruth Marshall Story
Teleplay by: Jean Holloway
Story by: Joe Stone & Paul King
Directed by: Richard Bartlett

Traveling through Sioux country, Flint McCullough agrees to help a man named Marshall find his daughter Ruth, taken by Native Americans in a raid many years before. In search of her, the scout is ambushed by a lone Indian. McCullough is rescued and treated by a blue-eyed white woman who lives with four wolves. Then Red Cloud, the Native American chief finds out that Flint is being treated by the "Woman Who Lives with Wolves" and orders him to be brought to his camp for punishment.

Ruth Marshall (Luana Patten), *Amos Marshall* (Mike Keene). *Ottie* (Fred Sherman), *Fleet Foot* (Sam Capuano).

#91. The Lita Foladaire Story
Teleplay by: Jean Holloway
Story by: Helen Cooper
Directed by: Jerry Hopper

Along the trail, Major Adams finds a woman unconscious and near death. He discovers she is the wife of his friend Jeff Foladaire. After she dies, Adams sets out to find the man responsible.

Lita Foladaire (Diane Brewster), *Dr. Cannon* (Tom Drake), *Jeff Foladaire* (Kent Smith), *Clay Foladaire* (Richard Crane), *Carlotti* (Jay Novello), *Mrs. Willoughby* (Lurene Tuttle), *Dan* (Paul Birch), *Mrs. Simmons* (Evelyn Brent).

#92. The Colonel Harris Story
Teleplay by: Gene L. Coon
Story by: Virgil Vogel & Gene L. Coon
Directed by: Virgil Vogel

Flint McCullough anxiously anticipates a visit with old friends at Fort Harris. Upon arrival at the fort, he finds his two close friends are about to start a senseless war.

Col. Harris (John Howard), *Bowman Lewis* (James Best), *Sgt. Boehmer* (Nestor Paiva), *Shegan* (Ken Mayer), *Princess* (Jacqueline DeWitt).

#93. The Marie Brant Story
Teleplay by: Milton Krims
Story by: Oliver Crawford
Directed by: Virgil Vogel

Orbio DaCosta, a wagon train traveler, meets widow Marie Brant and attempts to learn why she is distrustful of men, and has taught her son to be contemptuous of the weak and helpless.

Marie (Jean Hagen), *Orbio* (Edward Platt), *Matthew* (Richard Eyer), *Mrs. Taylor* (Claudia Bryar), *Simon* (Ronnie Sorensen).

#94. The Larry Hanify Story
Written by: Harold Swanton
Directed by: Ted Post

Before his death, Joe Hanify asks Flint McCullough to take care of his son Larry. McCullough agrees though he's warned that Larry is a liar and a thief.

Larry (Tommy Sands), *Callahan* (Gene Roth), *Aggie Donovan* (Cindy Robbins), *Marshall Kelleher* (Wally Moon), *McBee* (Olan Soule), *Mrs. Jurgis* (Edith Evanson), *Proprietor* (Joe Mell).

#95. The Clayton Tucker Story
Teleplay by: Thomas Thompson
Story by: George Shorling
Directed by: Virgil Vogel

A small party of travelers make their way through the desert to a rendezvous with Major Adams' wagon train. When their scout dies from a snake bite, the party must rely on one of their own to lead them.

Clayton Tucker (Jeff Morrow), *Sabrina Tucker* (Dorothy Green), *Art Bernard* (James Best), *Susan Bernard* (Aline Towne).

#96. The Benjamin Burns Story
Teleplay by: Gene L. Coon
Story by: Virgil Vogel & Gene L. Coon
Directed by: Virgil Vogel

A dried-up river leaves the wagon train short of water. Flint McCullough takes a group on a search for a legendary mountain spring with mountaineer guide Benjamin Burns. The men soon return and report that Burns has been killed and that Flint is responsible.

John Colter (James Franciscus), *Benjamin Burns* (J. Carrol Naish), *Kathy Burns* (Olive Sturgess), *Frank Owen* (Jack Lambert).

#97. The Ricky and Laurie Bell Story
Written & Directed by: Allan Miner

Ricky Bell, moving west with his family to start a new life, is jealous of all the attention his wife gives to their infant son.

Ricky Bell (James Gregory), *Laurie Bell* (June Lockart), *Jacob* (Theodore Newton), *Aunt Lizzie* (Ann Doran).

#98. The Tom Tuckett Story
Teleplay by: Jean Holloway
Based on Charles Dickens' *Great Expectations*
Directed by: Herschel Daugherty

A hunted traitor risks capture to see a youth who once helped him escape.

Nat Burkett (Robert Middleton), *Tom Tuckett* (Ben Cooper), *Miss Stevenson* (Josephine Hutchinson), *Elizabeth* (Louise Fletcher).

#99. The Tracy Sadler Story
Teleplay by: Norman Jolley
Story by: Norman Jolley & Eric Norden
Directed by: Ted Post

Tracy Sadler's son was born while she was in prison and then taken from her. After her release, she begins a search and finds he may be with the wagon train.

Tracy (Elaine Stritch), *Cadge Waldo* (Elisha Cook, Jr.), *Fletcher Forest* (Carl Benton Reid), *Arthur* (Eugene Martin).

#100. The Alexander Portlass Story
Written by: Leonard Praskins & Dick Nelson
Directed by: Jerry Hopper

An English archaeologist teams with an outlaw gang in search for Aztec treasure. When they need someone to guide them through the desert, they kidnap Flint.

A. Portlass (Peter Lorrie), *Jupe* (Morgan Woodward), *Bruto* (Bern Hoffman), *Latigo Kid* (Sherwood Price).

#101. The Christine Elliot Story
Written by: Jean Holloway
Directed by: Herschel Daugherty

A dozen boys seek to avoid an orphanage and join the wagon train. Traveler Christine Elliot is willing to help them escape but a state agency man is in close pursuit.

Christine Elliot (Phyllis Thaxter), *Phillip Ayers* (Donald Woods), *Mr. Snipple* (Henry Daniell), *George* (Don Grady).

#102. The Joshua Gilliam Story
Teleplay by: Gene L. Coon
Story by: Ralph Winters
Directed by: Virgil Vogel

On the trail, Major Adams finds Joshua Gilliam beaten and left for dead. Gilliam, a con man smells a new opportunity. He offers to be school teacher in return for passage.

Joshua (Dan Duryea), *Greta Halstadt* (Bethel Leslie), *Freda* (Irene Tedrow), *Sharon* (Betsy Brooks), *Mr. Miller* (Pitt Herbert).

#103. The Maggie Hamilton Story
Written & Directed by: Allen Miner

Maggie Hamilton, a spoiled young woman traveling on the wagon train rides off into the nearby hills, and plans to sulk until someone comes to find her. Someone does—a group of outlaws.

Maggie Hamilton (Susan Oliver), *H. J. Hamilton* (Les Tremayne), *Marie Louise Hamilton* (Sylvia Marriott), *Slim* (Orville Sherman), *Cherokee Ned* (Leonard Nimoy).

#104. The Jonas Murdock Story
Written by: Norman Jolley
Directed by: Virgil Vogel

Jonas Murdock, a rabbit-hunting mountaineer, creates problems for the wagon train by defying the no-hunting edict of a local Native American chief.

Jonas (Noah Berry, Jr.), *Red Hawk* (Joseph Barnett), *Alma Hardy* (Bernadette Withers), *Jameson* (Lyle Talbot), *Mrs. Jameson* (Gail Bonney).

#105. The Amos Gibbon Story
Written by: Gene L. Coon
Directed by: Joseph Pevney

Amos Gibbon and his gang have been taking prisoners and forcing them into slave trade. When they capture Flint McCullough, he tries to talk his fellow prisoners into escaping.

Amos Gibbon (Charles Aidman), *Judge Tremayne* (Arthur Shields), *Tom Duncan* (Francis J. McDonald), *Hank Morton* (Bob Hopkins).

#106. Trial for Murder *(Part One)*
Written by: Jean Holloway
Directed by: Virgil Vogel

A member of the wagon train is found clubbed to death, and overwhelming evidence points to the guilt of Brad Mason, a surly, friendless drunk.

Sir Alexander Drew (Henry Daniell), *Mark Applewhite* (Henry Hull), *Brad Mason* (Marshall Thompson), *Leslie Ivars* (Diane Foster), *Miller* (Murvyn Vye), *Elliot Drake* (William Schallert), *Eileen* (Melinda Plowman), *Molly Cassidy* (Connie Gilchrist).

#107. Trial for Murder *(Part Two)*
Written by: Jean Holloway
Directed by: Virgil Vogel

When Brad Mason is accused of murder, many on the train want to lynch him. Adams insists on a trial. Then Mason blurts out a confession and his conviction seems certain. Now the defense counsel produces a surprise witness, the dead man's wife.

Sir Alexander Drew (Henry Daniell), *Mark Applewhite* (Henry Hull), *Brad Mason* (Marshall Thompson), *Leslie Ivers* (Diane Foster), *Miller* (Murvyn Vye), *Eileen* (Melinda Plowman), *Elliot Drake* (William Schallert).

#108. The Countess Baranof Story
Teleplay by: Norman Jolley
Story by: Lee Karson
Directed by: Ted Post

Countess Baranof is in a hurry to reach Alaska before its rumored sale to the United States. She urges Flint to leave the train, guide her via a swifter route, and uses her feminine charm.

Countess (Taina Elg), *Col. Vasily* (Simon Oakland), *Alex Foster* (Peter Leeds), *Mrs. Foster* (Ann B. Davis).

#109. The Dick Jarvis Story
Written by: Floyd Burton
Directed by: Jerry Hopper

The Major takes a kindly interest in young Dick Jarvis who is fatherless and crippled. Then a runaway orphan youth joins the train and Dick feels his friendship with Adams is threatened.

Dick Jarvis (Tom Nolan), *Joey Henshaw* (Bobby Diamond), *Mrs. Jarvis* (Vivi Janiss), *Sam Hulsey* (Richard Reeves), *Bully* (Vaughn Meadows).

#110. The Dr. Swift Cloud Story
Written by: Floyd Burton
Directed by: Virgil Vogel

Swift Cloud (whom we first met in episode #66) comes home from medical school to discover his tribesman attacking the wagon train. The travelers refuse to accept his medical aid and his own people think he's a traitor.

Dr. Swift Cloud (Rafael Campos), *Straight Arrow* (Phillip Pine), *Dabbs Hargrove* (Brad Morrow), *Chief Fire Cloud* (Henry Brandon).

#111. The Luke Grant Story
Written by: Donald Gordon
Directed by: Christian Nyby

Friendly Mojave Native Americans find Luke Grant dying in the desert and bring him to the wagon train. A singer on the train named Victoria, recognizes Grant as a minister she once knew and cared for.

Luke Grant (Donald Woods), *Victoria* (Joan O'Brien),
Reverend Peters (James Bell), *Angie* (Marlene Willis),
Fay (Wende Wagner), *Sue* (Kay Elhardt).

#112. The Charlene Brenton Story
Written by: Floyd Burton
Directed by: Virgil Vogel

A stagecoach arrives in Apache Flats. Its only passengers are a dead woman and her infant daughter, alive and well.

Casey (Sean McClory), *Flo* (Jean Wiles), *Jim Brenton*
(Raymond Bailey), *Sheriff* (Harry Harvey, Sr.).

#113. The Sam Livingston Story
Written by: Harold Swanton
Directed by: Joseph Pevney

Sam Livingston arrives in Carson City, Nevada, with a fortune in gold and a plot for revenge. The object of his attention: the town banker, once his partner in a mining claim.

Sam (Charles Drake), *Cass Fleming* (Onslow Stevens), *Abigail*
(Barbara Eiler), *Hotel Clerk* (James Lydon).

#114. The Shad Bennington Story
Written by: Fred Cassidy
Directed by: Joseph Pevney

On the last lap of the trip to California, an itinerant medicine man joins the wagon train with a performing lion.

Shad (David Wayne), *Jenny* (Maggie Pierce), *Winfrey* (Charles Herbert), *Princess Fatima* (Laurie Mitchell), *Mrs. Teale* (Claire Carleton).

WAGON TRAIN
Season Four: 1960-1961

	Episode Titles	Air Dates
115.	Wagons Ho!	9/28/60
116.	The Horace Best Story	10/5/60
117.	The Albert Farnsworth Story	10/12/60
118.	The Allison Justis Story	10/19/60
119.	The Jose Morales Story	10/26/60
120.	Princess of a Lost Tribe	11/2/60
121.	The Cathy Eckhart Story	11/9/60
122.	The Bleymier Story	11/16/60
123.	The Colter Craven Story	11/23/60
124.	The Jane Hawkins Story	11/30/60
125.	The Candy O'Hara Story	12/7/60
126.	The River Crossing	12/14/60
127.	The Roger Bigelow Story	12/21/60
128.	The Jeremy Dow Story	12/28/60
129.	The Earl Packer Story	1/4/61
130.	The Patience Miller Story	1/11/61
131.	The Sam Elder Story	1/18/61
132.	Weight of Command	1/25/61
133.	The Prairie Story	2/1/61
134.	Path of the Serpent	2/8/61
135.	The Odyssey of Flint McCullough	2/15/61
136.	The Beth Pearson Story	2/22/61
137.	The Jed Polke Story	3/1/61
138.	The Nancy Palmer Story	3/8/61
139.	The Christopher Hale Story	3/15/61

Episode Titles	Air Dates
140. The Tiburcio Mendez Story	3/22/61
141. The Nellie Jefferson Story	4/5/61
142. The Saul Bevins Story	4/12/61
143. The Joe Muharich Story	4/19/61
144. The Duke Shannon Story	4/26/61
145. The Will Santee Story	5/3/61
146. The Jim Bridger Story	5/10/61
147. The Eleanor Culhane Story	5/17/61
148. The Chalice	5/24/61
149. The Janet Hale Story	5/31/61
150. Wagon to Fort Anderson	6/7/61
151. The Ah Chong Story	6/14/61
152. The Don Alvarado Story	6/21/61

#115. Wagons Ho!
Written by: Jean Holloway
Directed by: Herschel Daugherty

As the wagon train crew prepares to return to St. Joseph, MO, Flint shares the content of a book he read by Sam Evans, *The Greenhorn* who traveled with them a year before.

Samuel T. Evans (Mickey Rooney), *Aunt Em* (Ellen Corby), *Melanie Evans* (Olive Sturgess), *Black Feather* (Henry Corden).

#116. The Horace Best Story
Written by: Jean Holloway
Directed by: Jerry Hopper

Horace Best claims to be Major Adams' distant cousin, yet a far cry from the same sturdy stock. Nevertheless, he yearns to be a wagonmaster, which spells trouble for the Major.

Horace Best (George Gobel), *Pappy Lightfoot* (Ken Curtis), *Edwin Crook* (Joe Flynn), *Mr. Gillespie* (Allen Jenkins), *Mrs. Gillespie* (Mary Field).

#117. The Albert Farnsworth Story
Written by: Gene L. Coon
Directed by: Herschel Daugherty

Col. Albert Farnsworth, a British Army surgeon traveling with the wagon train, is convinced that the British way of life is the only way.

Farnsworth (Charles Laughton), *Mike O'Toole* (Terence de Marney), *Tim O'Toole* (Robert Brown), *Jeremy Oakes* (James Fairfax).

#118. The Allison Justis Story
Written by: Norman Jolley
Directed by: Ted Post

Flint shoots a horse thief named Justis, then learns the man was a respected mayor of the nearby town and husband of a former girlfriend.

Allison (Gloria DeHaven), *Billy Justis* (Michael Burns),
Ben Justis (Gregg Stewart), *Deputy* (Edward G. Robinson, Jr.),
Sheriff (Dan Tobin).

#119. The Jose Morales Story
Written by: Gene L. Coon
Directed by: Virgil Vogel

Bill Hawks leads three wagons across Sioux territory and gets captured by Jose Morales and his Mexican bandidos.

Morales (Lee Marvin), *Louis* (Lon Chaney, Jr.), *Raleigh* (Greg Palmer), *Patience* (Aline Towne), *Joseph* (Charles Herbert).

#120. Princess of a Lost Tribe
Written by: Jean Holloway
Directed by: Richard Whorf

When Flint and his companions discover descendants of an Aztec tribe living in a hidden city, they are told they cannot leave the ancient grounds.

Montezuma (Raymond Massey), *Lia* (Linda Lawson), *Mike Kelly* (Edward Mallory), *Jerald* (Raymond Greenleaf).

#121. The Cathy Eckhart Story
Teleplay by: Vince Giffoni & Sutton Roley
Story by: Vince Giffoni
Directed by: Sutton Roley

Adams plans to avoid a certain pass where several wagon trains have disappeared, but the alternative routes seem equally dangerous.
Cathy Eckhart (Susan Oliver), *Preacher* (Martin Landau), *Lieutenant* (Ron Hayes), *Sarah Harness* (Vivi Janiss), *Ben Harness* (John Larch), *Jeff Miller* (Gregory Walcott).

#122. The Bleymier Story
Teleplay by: William Raynor & Myles Wilder
Story by: Milton Krims
Directed by: Virgil Vogel

Flint guides a small party of settlers on their way to homesteads in the Dakota Territory. When they become bogged down by torrential rains, Samuel Bleymier claims the raging skies are an omen of catastrophe.

Bleymier (Dan Duryea), *Justin Claiborne* (James Drury), *Latch* (John McLiam), *Mrs. Cowan* (Juney Ellis).

#123. The Colter Craven Story
Teleplay by: Tony Paulson
Story by: John Ford
Directed by: John Ford

Major Adams and the wagon train come across the disabled wagon of Dr. Colter Craven and his wife. Though Craven, a former army physician, appears to be an alcoholic, Adams decides to give him a chance to become a useful member of the wagon train.

Colter Craven (Carleton Young), *Mrs. Craven* (Anna Lee), *General Ulysses Grant* (Paul Birch), *Jesse Grant* (Willis Bouchey), *Kyle* (Ken Curtis), *General William Sherman* (John Wayne), *Park Cleatus* (John Carradine), *Shelley* (Hank Worden), *Col. Lollier* (Richard Cutting), *Jamie* (Dennis Rush).

#124. The Jane Hawkins Story

Written by: Norman Jolley
Directed by: R. G. Springsteen

Flint finds Jane Hawkins, who's been shot, and brings her into the nearest town. The doctor there is reluctant to treat her, fearing reprisals, since she was shot by the hired gun of town dictator Ben Mattox.

Jane Hawkins (Myrna Fahey), *Ben Mattox* (Edgar Buchanan), *Jesse* (Sherwood Price), *Doc* (Whit Bissell), *Laura Mattox* (Kathie Browne), *Bartender* (Nestor Paiva).

#125. The Candy O'Hara Story

Written by: Harold Swanton
Directed by: Tay Garnett

Gabe Henry is anxious to remarry and provide a mother for his son Luther. He can't seem to find anyone suitable, but Luther spots Candy O'Hara on the street and feels she's the right one for both him and his father.

Candy O'Hara (Joan O'Brien), *Gabe Henry* (Jim Davis), *Luther* (Teddy Rooney), *Marshal* (Lane Bradford), *Marty* (Robert Lowery), *Parson* (Richard Cutting).

#126. The River Crossing

Written by: Jean Holloway
Directed by: Jesse Hibbs

When a river swells dangerously, Flint and Charlie Wooster find themselves left with half the wagon train on one side of the river, stuck between the raging tide and a Comanche war party.

Jabez Moore (Robert J. Wilke), *Col. Buckner* (Charles Aidman), *Lt. Beyins* (Ron Harper), *Tom* (Marshall Reed), *Pawnee Scout* (X. Brands).

#127. The Roger Bigelow Story
Written by: Floyd Burton
Directed by: Jerry Hopper

Clergyman Roger Bigelow and his wife Nancy travel to California with their life savings, intent on building a new church. The wagon train encounters wounded bandit Wes Varney, and the Bigelows offer him refuge and medical attention, despite Adams' warning that he's dangerous.

Roger Bigelow (Robert Vaughn), *Nancy Bigelow* (Audrey Dalton), *Wes Varney* (Claude Akins).

#128. The Jeremy Dow Story
Written by: Harold Swanton
Directed by: Virgil Vogel

Drifter Jeff Durant is hired to drive the Millikan's wagon west. Young Bruce Millikan travels with his mother Hester and stepfather Clete. When Bruce begins telling Durant about his real father, a supposed hero, Durant becomes very uncomfortable.

Jeff Durant (Leslie Nielsen), *Hester Millikan* (Mari Aldon), *Bruce Millikan* (Michael Burns), *Clete Millikan* (James Lydon), *Jubal* (Morgan Woodward).

#129. The Earl Packer Story
Written by: Gene L. Coon
Directed by: Sutton Roley

Sheriff Bill Strode who once saved Flint's life, has a reputation as a formidable lawman. Wounded, he asks for Flint's help. The scout is concerned as to why Strode is trying to elude Earl Packer, a determined and relentless bounty hunter.

Earl Packer (Ernest Borgnine), *Sheriff Bill Strode* (Ed Binns), *Harry* (Rex Holman).

#130. The Patience Miller Story
Written by: Jean Holloway
Directed by: Mitchell Leisen

The Millers, Quaker missionaries, travel west to the Arapahoe Indian Mission where they're attacked by hostile Native Americans. Patience Miller vows to continue the work of her slain husband and help the tribe.

> *Patience Miller* (Rhonda Fleming), *North Star* (Michael Ansara), *Dark Eagle* (Henry Brandon), *Spotted Horse* (Morgan Woodward), *White Hawk* (Jason Robards, Sr.), *Evening Star* (Bart Bradley).

#131. The Sam Elder Story
Written by: William Raynor & Myles Wilder
Directed by: Virgil Vogel

Former Army Captain Sam Elder asks Bill Hawks if he and his group of orphaned boys can join the train. Hawks agrees, but soon finds some wagon train members upset. They've discovered things about Elder's war record they don't like.

> *Sam Elder* (Everett Sloane), *Sgt. Perks* (Ray Stricklyn), *Millie Allen* (Roberta Shore), *Tod* (Roger Mobley), *Ben Allen* (Walter Coy), *Lila Allen* (Adrienne Marden).

#132. Weight of Command
Written by: Harold Swanton
Directed by: Herschel Daugherty

Bill Hawks and two men from the train investigate the ruins of an adobe hut, and get attacked by renegade Native Americans.

> *Duke Shannon* (Denny Miller), *Dan Foster* (Richard Crane), *George Gentry* (Dan Riss), *Bill Gentry* (Tommy Rettig), *Charlie* (Jan Arvin), *Hester Gentry* (Jeanne Bates), *Judith Foster* (Nancy Rennick), *Prudence* (Dana Dillaway), *Colonel* (Wilton Graff).

#133. The Prairie Story
Written by: Jean Holloway
Directed by: Mitchell Leisen

The wagon train women travelers endure the hardship of the arid prairie and threat of Indian attacks; then it becomes apparent that Charity Kirby is unwilling to face the dangers of the crossing.

Grandma (Beulah Bondi), *Charity Kirby* (Jan Clayton), *Clara* (Virginia Christine), *Matt* (John Archer), *Sally* (Diane Jergens), *Jack* (Jack Buetel), *Garth* (Mickey Sholdar).

#134. Path of the Serpent
Written by: Jean Holloway
Directed by: Virgil Vogel

Penelope, a young woman passenger, learns that her father is dying in a village just beyond an area of Indian uprisings. Ruddy Blaine, a mountaineer, offers to guide Penelope through a dangerous mountain trail to reach her father.

Ruddy Blaine (Noah Berry, Jr.), *Penelope* (Melinda Plowman), *The Serpent* (Jay Silverheels), *Sgt. Huntington* (Paul Birch), *Cpl. Clay Taylor* (Robert Harland).

#135. The Odyssey of Flint McCullough
Written by: Leonard Praskins & Sloan Nibley
Directed by: Frank Arrigo

Flint finds the survivors of an Indian raid, including a grandfather and a group of children. He decides to guide them out of the hostile territory surrounding them.

Gideon (Henry Hull), *Homer* (Michael Burns), *Kathy* (Suzie Carnell), *Cassie* (Dana Dillaway).

#136. The Beth Pearson Story
Written by: Norman Jolley
Directed by: Virgil Vogel

When widow Beth Pearson and her son Ronald join the train, Major Adams is strangely shaken by her presence. Beth closely resembles Ranie Webster, the woman Adams once loved. (This was the final appearance of Ward Bond as Wagonmaster Seth Adams.)

Beth Pearson (Virginia Grey), *Ronald* (Johnny Washbrook), *Johnson* (Del Moore).

#137. The Jed Polke Story
Written by: Peter Germano
Directed by: Virgil Vogel

McCullough finds Jed and Rheba Polke near death in the desert, but the only doctor on the train refuses to treat Jed.

Jed Polke (John Lasell), *Rheba Polke* (Joyce Meadows), *Keene* (Morgan Woodward), *Ross* (Ron Hayes), *Jeff* (Perry Lopez), *Otto* (Frank Gerstle).

#138. The Nancy Palmer Story
Written by: Theodore & Matilde Ferro
Directed by: John English

The wagon train travelers don't care for Dan Palmer and his unpleasant personality. Dan's wife Nancy offsets her husband's flaws with acts of kindness. Then a theft is discovered and the train members suspect Dan.

Dan Palmer (Jack Cassidy), *Nancy Palmer* (Audrey Meadows), *Lem Salters* (Elisha Cook, Jr.), *Freddie* (Roger Mobley), *Will Davidson* (Harry Lauter), *Mrs. MacGregor* (Jeanne Bates), *Mr. MacGregor* (Bern Hoffman), *Madge* (Vivi Janiss), *Sheriff Gile* (Med Florey), Doreen (Laurie Perreau).

#139. The Christopher Hale Story
Directed by: Herschel Daugherty

Flint meets Christopher Hale, a retired wagonmaster, overcome with grief after his family is massacred by Native Americans. Flint tries to persuade him to hire on as the new wagonmaster. Meanwhile the holding company who owns the wagon train employs a new wagonmaster, Jud Benedict, who arrives with four gunslingers to maintain order on the train.

Chris Hale (John McIntire), *Jud Benedict* (Lee Marvin), *Lenny* (L. Q. Jones), *Stevens* (Wesley Lau), *Wash* (Read Morgan), *Mrs. Stevens* (Nancy Rennick).

#140. The Tiburcio Mendez Story
Written by: Gene L. Coon
Directed by: David Lowell Rich

Bill Hawks leaves the train to guide four wagons southwest toward Los Angeles. On the way he's stopped by Tiburcio Mendez and his band of renegades who prevent him from entering California.

Tiburcio Mendez (Nehemiah Persoff), *Joaquin* (Leonard Nimoy), *Judge Alfred Black* (Russell Collins), *Alma* (Lisa Gaye), *Cross* (Lane Bradford).

#141. The Nellie Jefferson Story
Written by: Harold Swanton
Directed by: Virgil Vogel

Flint and new wagonmaster Chris Hale are annoyed by the demands of actress Nellie Jefferson, a new traveler. Wooster, though, is smitten and waits on Nellie hand and foot.

Nellie (Janis Paige), *Sean* (Don Megowan), *Bart Haskell* (H. M. Wynant), *Trader* (Hank Worden), *Homer* (Dennis Rush), *Marshal* (Don Harvey).

#142. The Saul Bevins Story
Written by: Jean Holloway
Directed by: Joseph Pevney

Saul Bevins, who is blind, must prove he is capable of caring for his son Job and sister Martha during the journey westward. Although he's been turned down by several wagonmasters, Chris Hale decides to give him a chance.

Saul Bevins (Rod Steiger), *Jane Harley* (Rachel Ames), *Job* (Charles Herbert), *Martha* (Vivi Janiss), *Jed* (I. Stanford Jolley).

#143. The Joe Muharich Story
Written by: Gene L. Coon

Kindly Polish immigrant Joe Muharich notices young Johnny Kamen has a bad attitude along with a fast gun. He decides to try and tame him before he runs into the wrong people, which Joe does himself.

Joe (Akim Tamiroff), *Johnny* (Robert Blake), *Whittaker* (Tris Coffin), *Betty Whittaker* (Susan Silo), *Sheriff* (Stacy Harris), *Jones* (Ken Mayer).

#144. The Duke Shannon Story
Written by: Norman Jolley
Directed by: Virgil Vogel

Duke Shannon (Denny Miller) has signed on to scout for the wagon train along with Flint McCullough. His grandfather, Henry Shannon, has a map for lost gold and talks Charles Wooster into joining him in recovering the treasure. Three men overhear the plan, trail the pair, and take the gold.

Henry Shannon (Frank McHugh), *Sterkel* (James Griffith), *Jeff* (John Cason), *Clay* (Leonard Geer), *Ethel* (Maudie Prickett).

#145. The Will Santee Story
Written by: Harold Swanton
Directed by: Ted Post

The Sheridan family joins the wagon train then confides in Hale that their real name is Santee, and they use an alias because one family member was involved in a scandal.

Will (Dean Stockwell), *Jessie McDermott* (Millie Perkins), *Agnes* (Jocelyn Brando), *Fred McDermott* (Harry Von Zell), *Stranger* (John Crawford), *Lee* (Dal McKennon).

#146. The Jim Bridger Story
Written by: Jean Holloway
Directed by: David Butler

Flint McCullough, temporarily in charge, is ordered by Army General Jameson to take the train back into hostile territory to rescue a trapped cavalry garrison.

Jim Bridger (Karl Swenson), *General Jameson* (John Doucette), *Gray Beddoe* (Hank Brandt), *Mavis Beddoe* (Jackie Russell), *Sgt. Hoag* (Nestor Paiva), *Captain Fox* (Glen Strange).

#147. The Eleanor Culhane Story
Written by: Gene L. Coon
Directed by: Ted Post

Flint visits Eleanor Culhane, an old flame, and now a reclusive widow. As he coaxes her to return to the world, he finds his love for her returning. Unfortunately, so does her dead husband.

Eleanor (Felicia Farr), *Riker Culhane* (John Lasell), *Harris* (Russell Thorson), *Old Man* (Hank Patterson).

#148. The Chalice
Written by: William Raynor & Miles Wilder
Directed by: Virgil Vogel

The Canevaris family heads for California to plant a new vineyard, and need help to transport water to keep the grapevines alive during the journey. Two men, Carstairs and Barker, offer them the use of their wagon but their gesture isn't unselfish as they figure out what they can take back from the Canevaris family.

> *Carstairs* (Lon Chaney), *Barker* (Richard Jaeckel), *Lisa Canevaris* (Angela Brunetti), *Marcello Canevaris* (Harold Heifetz), Padre (Edward Colemans).

#149. The Janet Hale Story
Written by: Norman Jolley

In a flashback, Chris Hale's duties as wagonmaster require him to leave his family in their prairie home. His truce with Red Cloud reassures him there won't be any danger from Indian raids.

> *Janet Hale* (Jeanette Nolan), *Whit Martin* (Charles Aidman), *Helen Martin* (Bethel Leslie).

#150. Wagon to Fort Anderson
Written by: Peter Germano
Directed by: Ted Post

Flint finds Fay and Sue Ellison, two survivors of a Native American massacre, but his attempt to lead them to safety is jeopardized by two army deserters who tell the girls Flint is leading them to disaster.

> *George* (Albert Salmi), *Joe* (Don Rickles), *Sam Livingston* (Charles Drake), *Fay Ellison* (Carol Rossen), *Sue Ellison* (Candy Moore), *Warrior* (Hal Needham).

#151. The Ah Chong Story
Teleplay by: Sheldon Bonnewell
Story by: Terry Wilson
Directed by: Virgil Vogel

Wooster has developed a take-it-or-leave-it attitude with regard to his cooking, so Hale and Hawks decide to leave it and promote Wooster's Chinese helper to chief cook for the wagon train.

Ah Chong (Arnold Stang), *Sheriff* (Frank Ferguson).

#152. The Don Alvarado Story
Written by: Jean Holloway
Directed by: David Butler

Flint promises a dying Spanish nobleman help, and impersonates Don Alvarado to claim his inheritance for the rest of his family.

Teresa (Andra Martin), *Felipe* (Vladimir Sokoloff), *Maria* (Minerva Urecal), *Julio* (Michael Forest), *Donovan* (Ed Nelson).

WAGON TRAIN
Season Five: 1961-1962

Episode Titles	Air Dates
153. The Captain Dan Brady Story	9/27/61
154. The Kitty Albright Story	10/4/61
155. The Maud Frazier Story	10/11/61
156. The Selena Hartnell Story	10/18/61
157. The Clementine Jones Story	10/25/61
158. The Jenna Douglas Story	11/1/61
159. The Artie Matthewson Story	11/8/61
160. The Mark Miner Story	11/15/61
161. The Bruce Saybrook Story	11/22/61
162. The Lizabeth Ann Calhoun Story	12/6/61
163. The Traitor	12/13/61
164. The Bettina Mae Story	12/20/61
165. Clyde	12/27/61
166. The Martin Onyx Story	1/3/62
167. The Dick Pederson Story	1/10/62
168. The Hobie Redman Story	1/17/62
169. The Malachi Hobart Story	1/24/62
170. The Dr. Denker Story	1/31/62
171. The Lonnie Fallon Story	2/7/62
172. The Jeff Hartfield Story	2/14/62
173. The Daniel Clay Story	2/21/62
174. The Lieutenant Burton Story	2/28/62
175. The Charley Shutup Story	3/7/62
176. The Amos Billings Story	3/14/62
177. The Baylor Crowfoot Story	3/21/62

Episode Titles	Air Dates
178. The George B. Hanrahan Story	3/28/62
179. The Swamp Devil	4/4/62
180. The Cole Crawford Story	4/11/62
181. The Levi Hale Story	4/18/62
182. The Terry Morrell Story	4/25/62
183. The Jud Steele Story	5/2/62
184. The Mary Beckett Story	5/9/62
185. The Nancy Davis Story	5/16/62
186. The Frank Carter Story	5/23/62
187. The John Turnball Story	5/30/62
188. The Hiram Winthrop Story	6/6/62
189. The Heather Mahoney Story	6/13/62

#153. The Captain Dan Brady Story
Written by: Gene L. Coon

Chris Hale faces a serious dilemma. If he hires Dan Brady, who demands to be taken on as the train's scout, he'll lose Flint McCullough. If he doesn't, he'll lose a Government mail contract that will finance the wagon train.

Captain Dan Brady (Joseph Cotton), *John Grey Cloud* (Paul Comi), *Murray* (David Faulkner), *Mrs. Murray* (Dawn Wells), *Major* (Russell Thorson), *Brown* (Edward Colemans).

#154. The Kitty Albright Story
Written by: Norman Jolley

Nurse Kitty Albright becomes concerned about the poor sanitation habits of her fellow travelers. When she tries to solve the problem, she finds the wagon members grossly misinformed about the nursing profession.

Kitty (Polly Bergen), *Lettie* (Jocelyn Brando), *Barney* (Morgan Woodward), *Lolly* (Kathleen Freeman), *Father Albright* (Howard Wendell), *Mother Albright* (Eleanor Audley).

#155. The Maud Frazier Story
Teleplay by: Rip Van Ronkel & Normal Jolley
Story by: Rip Von Ronkel

Flint encounters an all-woman wagon train led by Maud Frazier. He tries to persuade her not to lead her defenseless train into hostile Indian territory. She refuses and tries to persuade Flint to leave his train and come with hers.

Maud (Barbara Stanwyck), *Bessie* (Nora Marlowe).

#156. The Selena Hartnell Story
Written by: William Raynor & Myles Wilder

Female bounty hunter Selena Hartnell reaches the wagon train and tells Chris Hale to formally arrest traveler Will Cotrell, the beloved leader of a band of pacifists.

Selena (Jan Sterling), *Will Cotrell* (Claude Akins).

#157. The Clementine Jones Story
Written by: Harold Swanton
Directed by: David Lowell Rich

Clementine Jones is a popular performer at the local saloon who offends the town residents. When they complain to the Mayor, he expels her from the community. The wagon train is passing through and Hale offers Clementine passage west.

Clementine (Ann Blyth), *Willy Pettigrew* (Dick York), *Homer* (Roger Mobley), *Frank* (Henry Corden), *Gip* (Nestor Paiva).

#158. The Jenna Douglas Story
Teleplay by: John McGreevey
Story by: Peggy & Lou Shaw

The wagon train happens upon a woman stumbling along the trail and Chris Hale takes her in as a passenger. She tells him her name is Jenna Douglas but she doesn't reveal she's escaped from a mental hospital.

Jenna (Carolyn Jones), *Dr. David Miller* (John Lupton), *Ed Linders* (Charlie Briggs), *Henry Brandt* (Andy Green).

#159. The Artie Matthewson Story
Written by: Thomas Thompson

Flint discovers his foster brother has become the mayor of a boom town. He suspects the opportunistic Artie is up to no good but no one will believe him.

Artie (Rory Calhoun), *Angie* (Jane Darwell), *Melanie* (Joyce Meadows).

#160. The Mark Miner Story
Written by: Norman Jolley

The wagon train members suspect someone is stealing their belongings and all evidence points to Duke Shannon.

Mark Miner (Brandon DeWilde), *Matthew Miner* (Michael Burns), *Rev* (Robert Cornthwaite), *Eve* (Barbara Parkins).

#161. The Bruce Saybrook Story
Written by: Peter Germano

McCullough meets a group of British noblemen and warns them that they are right in the middle of hostile Indian territory.

Lord Bruce Saybrook (Brian Aherne), *Diana Saybrook* (Antoinette Bower), *Tommy* (Liam Sullivan).

#162. The Lizabeth Ann Calhoun Story
Written by: Norman Jolley

Lizabeth Ann Calhoun wants to join the train and begins flirting alternatively with Hawks and Shannon. Soon a jealous rivalry develops between the two friends.

Lizabeth (Dana Wynter), *Major Henley* (Raymond Bailey), *Lon Harper* (Richard Crane), *Ladron* (Peter Whitney).

#163. The Traitor
Written by: Norman Jolley
Directed by: Dick Moder

Flint McCullough, accused of being involved in a horse theft, is tried and found guilty by Chris Hale. His sentence is a whipping and banishment from the wagon train.

Sam Upton (Nick Adams), *Madge Upton* (Jeanne Cooper), *Sgt. Oakes* (Myron Healey), *Major Hansen* (Stacy Keach, Sr.), *Muerte* (Anthony Caruso).

#164. The Bettina May Story
Written & Directed by: Allen Miner

Chris Hale is not pleased when Bettina May and her large family join the wagon train. May pampers her children and Hale doesn't feel they can measure up to the rigors of the journey west.

Bettina May (Bette Davis), *Nathan May* (Joby Baker), *Gene* (Ron Hayes), *Rose* (Asa Maynor).

#165. Clyde
Written by: Gene L. Coon

Wooster develops an attachment to a captured buffalo at a time when the wagon train has a meat shortage.

Jan Sherman (Harry Von Zell), *Mrs. Sherman* (Lenore Kingston), *Sonny* (Michael McGreevey), *Arapahoe Chief* (Frank DeKova).

#166. The Martin Onyx Story
Written by: Robert Yale Libott

Martin Onyx, a legendary lawman, comes to the aid of a prairie town plagued by an outlaw gang. McCullough is suspicious. He was told Onyx was dead.

Martin Onyx (Jack Warden), *First Outlaw* (Sherwood Price),

Second Outlaw (Morgan Woodward), *Angus Breck* (Rhys Williams), *Jebediah* (Jack Albertson).

#167. The Dick Pederson Story

Teleplay by: Leonard Praskins
Story by: Marje Blood

Orphan Dick Pederson resents the other young people on the wagon train, particularly Janey Cutler, because they all have families. When Janey's four younger sisters befriend Dick, his attitude begins to change.

Dick Pederson (James McArthur), *Janey Cutler* (Anne Helm), *Mrs. Cutler* (Alice Frost).

#168. The Hobie Redman Story

Written by: Thomas Thompson

Duke Shannon is sent to guide three wagons waiting to join the train, but faces difficulty. Hobie Redman refuses to come along because his family died on the same trail a few years earlier.

Hobie (Lin McCarthy), *Glen Andrews* (Arch Johnson), *Ruth Carlson* (Barbara Eiler), *Clyde Montgomery* (Parley Baer), *Sandra* (Ann Jillian), *Agnes* (Amzie Strickland).

#169. The Malachi Hobart Story

Written by: Ken Kolb
Directed by: David Butler

Duke discovers that traveling preacher Malachi Hobart is really a con artist. To expose him, Duke pretends to be a victim of one of Hobart's schemes.

Malachi (Franchot Tone), *Martha Gresham* (Irene Ryan), *Roy Standish* (Steven Darrell), *George Gresham* (Wally Brown).

#170. The Dr. Denker Story
Written by: Steven Ritch & William Douglas Lansford
Directed by: Frank Arrigo

Flint finds young Billy Latham paralyzed with fear and unable to talk after witnessing the murder of his father.

Billy (Michael Burns), *Dr. Denker* (Theodore Bikel),
Ed Beaufort (George Keymas), *Emma Beaufort* (Kathleen O'Malley), *George Blair* (James Lydon).

#171. The Lonnie Fallon Story
Written by: Harold Swanton

Martin Jennings disapproves of young cowboy Lonnie Fallon, the suitor of his daughter Kathy. Jennings warns Fallon he will shoot him if he attempts to follow the wagon train.

Lonnie Fallon (Gary Clarke), *Kirby* (Alan Hale, Jr.), *Kathy Jennings* (Lynn Loring), *Martin Jennings* (Frank Overton), *Sheriff Fancher* (Stacy Harris).

#172. The Jeff Hartfield Story

Young Jeff Hartfield's father is in prison awaiting execution, so Jeff plans to run away from the train and save his father.

Jeff (Jack Chaplain), *Davey Adams* (Dennis Rush), *Steve Brewster* (Roger Mobley), *Dallas* (Michael Forest), *Link Hartfield* (House Peters, Jr.).

#173. The Daniel Clay Story
Written by: Steven Ritch

Daniel Clay, a judge with a reputation for giving harsh sentences, is disliked by the other travelers on the wagon train.

Daniel Clay (Claude Rains), *John Cole* (Fred Beir), *Frances Cole* (Maggie Pierce), *Margaret Clay* (Frances Reid), *Ethan Clay* (Peter Helm).

#174. The Lieutenant Burton Story
Teleplay by: Steven Ritch
Story by: Ken Kolb

Chris Hale is shot by a cavalry patrol searching for deserters. The order to shoot was given by impulsive Sergeant Kile who believes in shooting first and asking questions later.

Lt. Burton (Dean Jones), *Sgt. Kile* (Charles McGraw), *Danny Maitland* (Ray Stricklyn).

#175. The Charley Shutup Story
Written by: Gene L. Coon

Chris Hale and Duke Shannon escort a group from the wagon train through rugged snowy mountain country. When Duke breaks his leg, Hale and the others are forced to leave him behind with a wounded Native American.

Charley Shutup (Dick York), *John Muskie* (R. G. Armstrong), *Ethel Muskie* (Dorothy Green).

#176. The Amos Billings Story
Written by: Peter Germano

While scouting ahead of the wagon train, Flint McCullough encounters Amos Billings. Billings claims he and his son Gabe have blasted a road through a dead-end canyon that will save the wagons two weeks of travel.

Amos (Paul Fix), *Gabe* (Jon Locke), *Corso* (Greg Palmer), *John Anders* (Dennis Patrick), *Loan* (Jenny Engstrom).

#177. The Baylor Crowfoot Story
Teleplay by: John McGreevey
Story by: Prentiss Combs

Jethro Creech, a stern disciplinarian, catches schoolteacher Baylor Crowfoot exchanging glances with his daughter Ruth and warns Crowfoot to leave her alone.

Baylor (Robert Culp), *Jethro Creech* (John Larch), *Ruth Creech* (Joyce Taylor), *Emeterio* (Leonard Nimoy).

#178. The George B. Hanrahan Story
Written by: Gene L. Coon

Duke Shannon rescues Indian medicine man Running Bear from his fellow tribesmen and brings him to the wagon train. There he makes friends with politician George Hanrahan who thinks they will make a great team at conning the public.

Hanrahan (Lee Tracy), *Running Bear* (Frank DeKova), *Tim Hogan* (Harry Carey, Jr.), *Charlie Haynes* (Douglas Jones).

#179. Swamp Devil
Written by: Norman Jolley

Flint McCullough guides Otto Burger and his followers. When they arrive at the edge of a swamp, a friendly Native American chief advises them to detour, because an evil spirit dwells in the marshes ahead.

Otto Burger (Otto Waldis), *Joshua* (Phillip Bourneuf), *Bear Claw* (Robert Bice), *Mr. Harris* (Richard Cutting).

#180. The Cole Crawford Story
Written by: Thomas Thompson

Shortly after newlyweds Cole and Helen Crawford join the wagon train, Blake Dorty, a former suitor of Helen's, approaches the train and demands that Helen go away with him.

Cole Crawford (James Drury), *Helen Crawford* (Diana Millay), *Blake Dorty* (Robert Colbert).

#181. The Levi Hale Story
Written by: Leonard Praskins

Chris Hale journeys to a Wyoming prison to meet his older brother Levi who is being released. Hales thinks his brother has been pardoned, until the Warden tells him that Levi is being released on the condition that he leave the territory.

Levi Hale (John McIntire), *Warden* (Hugh Sanders), *Pete Rudge* (Trevor Bardette), *Deputy* (Myron Healey).

#182. The Terry Morrell Story
Written by: Peter Germano

Ben Morrell and his son Terry join the train and quickly establish themselves as anti-social people. In fact, Terry doesn't even seem to like his father.

Terry (David Ladd), *Ben Morrell* (Henry Jones), *Letty Morse* (Vivi Janiss), *Ralph Morse* (Paul Langton), *Zeb Landrus* (Lane Bradford).

#183. The Jud Steele Story
Written by: Peter Germano

Jud Steele, a fleeing gunman, shows up at the wagon train with a companion requesting fresh horses. Steele is displeased when Bill Hawks refuses.

Jud (Ed Binns), *Nathan Forge* (Arthur Franz), *Wesley Thomas* (Robert Wilke), *Simmons* (Cliff Osmond).

#184. The Mary Beckett Story
Teleplay by: Steven Ritch
Story by: Paul Hayward

Alex Lamont, a suave Frenchman, produces a mixed reaction among the travelers. The women adore him but the men believe he's a phony.

Mary Beckett (Anne Jeffreys), *Alex Lamont* (Lee Begere), *Frank Lane* (Whit Bissell), *Martha Lane* (Jocelyn Brando), *Robert Waring* (Joe Maross).

#185. The Nancy Davis Story
Written by: Steven Ritch

Flint McCullough, Bill Hawks and Charlie Wooster are in a local saloon when they hear the name Lace Andrews. Flint has been looking for Andrews for years. He holds him responsible for the death of a former girlfriend, and the wagon train scout has sworn to kill him. (The final appearance of Robert Horton in the series.)

Nancy Davis (Lory Patrick), *Loretta* (Cloris Leachman), *Lace Andrews* (Keith Richards), *Doc Shaw* (Russell Collins).

#186. The Frank Carter Story
Written by: Steven Ritch

Duke Shannon is a dead ringer for gambler Jason Carter. In fact, some people are convinced that Duke is Jason, including someone who plans to kill the gambler.

Frank Carter (Albert Salmi), *Mary Carter* (Frances Reid), *Martha* (Gloria Talbott), *Cyrus* (Edward Platt).

#187. The John Turnball Story
Written by: Gene L. Coon

White settlers are attempting to force Native Americans off their lands. However, this time they're faced with a legal barrier initiated by two attorneys named Jacob Solomon and John Turnball who returned from the East to help his fellow Indians.

John Turnball (Henry Silva), *Jack Thome* (Warren Stevens), *Jacob Solomon* (Steven Geray), *T. J. Gingle* (Dayton Lummis), *Nah-Ah-Kanay* (John War Eagle).

#188. The Hiram Winthrop Story
Written by: Peter Germano

Indian agent Hiram Winthrop persuades Duke Shannon to give up his job as wagon scout and help him establish a welfare program in his district.

Hiram (Eduard Franz), *Chief Two Arrows* (Ron Soble), *Jessica* (Barbara Woodell), *Lafe Riatt* (Art Lund), *Mary Carter* (Claudia Bryar), *Frank Carter* (Frank Gerstle).

#189. The Heather Mahoney Story
Written by: Norman Jolley

The wagon train reaches the end of the line in Sacramento. However, it might be a new beginning for Chris Hale when he becomes interested in widow Heather Mahoney.

Heather (Jane Wyatt), *Mother O'Hara* (Nellie Burt), *Harry* (John Emery), *Jamison* (Cyril Delevanti).

WAGON TRAIN
Season Six: 1962-1963

Episode Titles	Air Dates
190. The Wagon Train Mutiny	9/19/62
191. The Caroline Casteel Story	9/26/62
192. The Madame Sagittarius Story	10/3/62
193. The Martin Gatsby Story	10/10/62
194. The John Augustus Story	10/17/62
195. The Mavis Grant Story	10/24/62
196. The Lisa Raincloud Story	10/31/62
197. The Shiloh Degnan Story	11/7/62
198. The Levy-McGowan Story	11/14/62
199. The John Bernard Story	11/21/62
200. The Kurt Davos Story	11/28/62
201. The Eve Newhope Story	12/5/62
202. The Orly French Story	12/12/62
203. The Donna Fuller Story	12/19/62
204. The Sam Darland Story	12/26/62
205. The Abel Weatherly Story	1/2/63
206. The Davey Baxter Story	1/9/63
207. The Johnny Masters Story	1/16/63
208. The Naomi Kaylor Story	1/30/63
209. The Hollister John Garrison Story	2/6/63
210. The Lily Legend Story	2/13/63
211. Charlie Wooster—Outlaw	2/20/63
212. The Sara Proctor Story	2/27/63
213. The Emmett Lawton Story	3/6/63
214. The Annie Duggan Story	3/13/63

Episode Titles	*Air Dates*
215. The Michael McGoo Story	3/20/63
216. The Adam Mackenzie Story	3/27/63
217. The Tom Tuesday Story	4/3/63
218. Heather and Hamish	4/10/63
219. The Blane Wessels Story	4/17/63
220. The Tom O'Neal Story	4/24/63
221. The Clarence Mullins Story	5/1/63
222. The David Garner Story	5/8/63
223. Alias Bill Hawks	5/15/63
224. The Antone Rose Story	5/22/63
225. The Jim Whitlow Story	5/29/63
226. The Barnaby West Story	6/5/63

#190. The Wagon Train Mutiny
Written by: Norman Jolley
Directed by: Virgil Vogel

The wagon train finds a devastated wagon party with a wounded member of the attacking Comancheros who was left to die by his comrades. The wounded Comanchero warns Hale of an impending attack on his train.

> *Amos* (Dan Duryea), *Hannah* (Jane Wyman), *Renaldo* (Jose DeVega), *Leland* (Peter Helm), *Mr. Hunter* (Regis Toomey) *John Hunter* (Dick Jones).

#191. The Caroline Casteel Story
Written by: Gerry Day

Caroline Casteel was captured by Native Americans years ago. Frank Casteel has given up hope that his wife is still alive, then a man claims he has managed to trade her away from her abductors.

> *Caroline Casteel* (Barbara Stanwyck), *Frank Casteel* (Charles Drake), *Jamie Casteel* (Roger Mobley), *Scofield* (Robert F. Simon).

#192. The Madame Sagittarius Story
Written by: Leonard Praskins
Directed by: Virgil Vogel

A close relationship develops between Charlie Wooster and Madame Sagittarius, a supposed con woman, snubbed by the rest of the wagon train passengers.

> *Madame Sagittarius* (Thelma Ritter), *Dennie Hallock* (Doug Lambert), *Jeb Morgan* (Murvyn Vye).

#193. The Martin Gatsby Story
Written by: Thomas Thompson

Martin Gatsby, a wealth merchant, wants the wagons to keep moving. He's become impatient with Caleb Lefton causing delays and tells Hale the Lefton family should leave the wagon train.

Gatsby (Fred Clark), *Elaine Gatsby* (Virginia Christine), *Jeb* (Harry Carey, Jr.), *Caleb* (James McCallion), *Grace* (Jocelyn Brando).

#194. The John Augustus Story

John Augustus plays cards with Chinese merchant Din Pau Yee and wins an unusual prize: a beautiful Chinese girl named Mayleen.

John (Joseph Cotton), *Mayleen* (Nobu McCarthy), *Din Pau* Yee (Allen Jung), *Matilda* (Meg Wyllie).

#195. The Mavis Grant Story

The wagon train is in desperate need of water. Well owner Mavis Grant offers them all they need but for an astronomical price.

Mavis (Ann Sheridan), *Maitland* (Parley Baer), *Mrs. Maitland* (Anna Karen).

#196. The Lisa Raincloud Story
Teleplay by: Steven Ritch
Story by: Dana Wynter & Steven Ritch

Bill Hawks is badly wounded and taken prisoner by Native Americans who plan to execute him as soon as he recovers. During his convalescence, Hawks and Indian Princess Lisa Raincloud fall in love.

Lisa (Dana Wynter), *Grey Wolf* (George Keymas), *Tabor* (Gregg Barton), *Jethro* (Dal McKennon), *Pearson* (Ken Mayer).

#197. The Shiloh Degnan Story
Written by: Harold Swanton

Chris Hale finds Major Dan Marriott, a badly wounded soldier near the wagon train's campsite. Before he dies, Marriott accuses Shiloh Degnan, his commanding officer and a national hero, of murder by sending him to certain death in a battle with Native Americans.

Major Dan Marriott (Russell Johnson), *Mrs. Marriott* (Nancy Gates), *Shiloh Degnan* (Lorence Kerr), *Gen. Kirby* (R.G. Armstrong), *Fogarty* (Barry Morse), *McClellan* (James Gavin), *Galloway* (Peter Whitney).

#198. The Levy-McGowan Story
Written by: Bob Barbash

The feud between travelers Simon Levy and Patrick McGowan makes it difficult for McGowan's son Sean to carry on his romance with Levy's daughter Rachel.

Patrick McGowan (Liam Redmond), *Simon Levy* (Leo Fuchs), *Rachel Levy* (Lory Patrick), *Sean McGowan* (Gary Vinson).

#199. The John Bernard Story
Written by: John Kneubuhl

Native Americans kidnap Mrs. Budgeon, a traveler on the wagon train, and leave Mitsina, one of their own, who is seriously ill. They promise to return Mrs. Budgeon when Mitsina is cured.

John Bernard (Robert Ryan), *Mitsina* (Perry Lopez), *Ben* (Cliff Osmond), *Larry* (Beau Bridges), *Budgeon* (William Fawcett).

#200. The Kurt Davos Story
Written by: Ted Sherdeman

Florence Hastings, a wagon train passenger, fears dogs and avoids fellow traveler Kurt Davos and his bulldog. Then a wild bull charges Florence and it's Kurt and his dog who come to the rescue.

Kurt (Eddie Albert), *Florence Hastings* (Frances Reid), *Will Hershey* (Arthur Space), *Minnie Hershey* (Amzie Strickland).

#201. The Eve Newhope Story
Written by: John McGreevey

Patrick O'Shaughnessy travels west to surprise his respectable, married daughter. To his surprise, his daughter Eve isn't married and runs a saloon.

Patrick (Tudor Owen), *Eve* (Ann Blyth), *Dan Ryan* (Jim Davis), *Orv Bassett* (Richard Reeves), (Slim Pickens).

#202. The Orly French Story
Written by: Norman Jolley
Directed by: Virgil Vogel

Marshall Jason Hartman has become deeply religious. When he meets up with young bank robber Orly French, he tries to instill faith and kindness in the boy.

Jason Hartman (John Doucette), *Orly French* (Peter Fonda), *Judy* (Sharon Farrell), *Dr. Wilson* (Robert Cornthwaite), *Bates* (Gil Perkins).

#203. The Donna Fuller Story
Written by: Norman Jolley

Temperance worker Donna Fuller and a group of female followers join the wagon train. Then Donna falls for Alonzo Galezio and to her chagrin, discovers he's a wine maker.

Donna (Jeanne Cooper), *Alonzo* (Simon Oakland), *Edith* (Sandra Gould), *Dolly* (Kathleen Freeman).

#204. The Sam Darland Story
Teleplay by: Steven Ritch & Walter Wagner
Story by: Walter Wagner

The wagon train comes across Sam Darland who has started a home for a group of orphan boys in an abandoned town in the middle of Indian country.

Sam (Art Linkletter), *Mrs. Baxter* (Nancy Davis), *Billy* (Tommy Nolan), *Toddy* (Billy Mumy), *Tulo* (X Brands).

#205. The Abel Weatherly Story
Written by: Robert Yale Libott

Bill Hawks and Charles Wooster find an overturned wagon on the prairie and give aid to injured Abel Weatherly, a sea captain. Then during the night, Weatherly goes into a violent rage and tries to kill Hawks.

Abel Weatherly (J.D. Cannon), *Fratelli* (John Ashley), *Drifter* (William Fawcett).

#206. The Davey Baxter Story
Written by: Pat Fielder

Davey Baxter loses his mother in a wagon accident that also mangles his arm. The doctor is away and Chris Hale must decide if Davey's arm should be amputated to save his life.

Davey Baxter (Tommy Sands), *Susan* (Jeannine Riley), *Walley* (Charles Herbert), *Forks* (Sam Edwards), *Mrs. Forbes* (Louise Arthur).

#207. The Johnny Masters Story
Written by: Peter Germano

Enroute to Fort David to get a miliary escort for the wagons, Duke Shannon rescues Indian-turned-soldier Johnny Masters from a war party. They arrive at the Fort, but find the troopers on patrol.

Johnny Masters (Anthony George), *Col. Stone* (Robert Wilkie), *Capt. Sanborn* (Harry Hickox), *Waters* (William Mims), *Bledsoe* (Alvy Moore), *Flynn* (Kelly Thordsen).

#208. The Naomi Kaylor Story
Written by: William Raynor & Myles Wilder
Directed by: Bernard Gerard

Naomi Kaylor accepts her husband's death calmly until she learns that he left most of his estate to her step-daughter.

Naomi (Joan Fontaine), *Grace* (Natalie Trundy), *Tom* (Dick Sargent), *Blucher* (Fred Beir).

#209. The Hollister John Garrison Story
Written by: Gene L. Coon

Stevenson Drake, a bitter ex-Confederate soldier, has a strong dislike for Southerner Hollister Garrison who didn't fight for the Confederacy.

Garrison (Charles Drake), *Drake* (Gary Cockrell), *Melody* (Evans Evans), *Kempton* (Peter Whitney).

#210. The Lily Legend Story
Written by: Leonard Praskins & Sloan Nibley

Duke Shannon meets Lily Legend, his childhood sweetheart, being escorted by a Sheriff on the way to her hanging.

Lily (Susan Oliver), *Piper* (Richard Jaeckel), *Sheriff Lund* (Trevor Burdette).

#211. Charley Wooster—Outlaw
Written by: Leonard Praskins

In an attempt to find the location of a gold shipment carried by the wagon train, bandit Bella McKavitch has her two sons kidnap Chris Hale; but the boys get confused and take Wooster instead.

Bella (Jeanette Nolan), *Esdras* (L. Q. Jones), *Ciel* (Morgan Woodward), *Sheriff* (Frank Ferguson), *Scotty* (Mickey Sholdar).

#212. The Sarah Proctor Story
Written by: Leonard Praskins

The wagon train members believe Sarah Proctor mutilated dolls belonging to the children, and feel she is mentally ill.

Sarah (Jean Hagen), *Brad* (Chris Robinson), *Jenny* (Holly McIntire).

#213. The Emmett Lawton Story
Written by: Gene L. Coon

In the town of High Times, scout Duke Shannon kills a hired gunman in self-defense, then faces the wrath of the town ruler.

Emmett Lawton (Dennis Hopper), *Mrs. Lawton* (Frances Reid), *Perk Lopely* (Richard Devon), *Jed* (Ric Roman), *Monte West* (Stanley Adams), *Del Masters* (Rusty Lane).

#214. The Annie Duggan Story
Teleplay by: John McGreevey
Story by: Gary Munn

An elderly couple on the train die of typhoid fever and their servant Annie Duggan is quarantined. Despite the widespread concern among the passengers, Dan Highet is annoyed that the woman he loves has been sequestered.

Annie (Carolyn Kearney), *Dan Highet* (Arthur Franz).

#215. The Michael McGoo Story
Written by: Norman Jolley

Charlie Wooster wants to adopt four orphaned brothers so he proposes to traveler Ada Meyers.

Ada (Jocelyn Brando), *Michael McGoo* (John Doucette), *Humphrey* (Roger Mobley), *Mrs. Lawson* (Cathleen Cordell).

#216. The Adam MacKenzie Story
Written by: Norman Jolley

A physician and his family are run off their land by an angry mob, which accuses the daughter of being a witch.

Adam MacKenzie (Michael Ansara), *Benedict O'Brien* (Peter Brown), *Felipe Perez* (Danny Bravo), *Juana* (Lois Roberts), *Estaban* (William Mims).

#217. The Tom Tuesday Story
Written by: Leonard Praskins and Sloan Nibley

Outlaw Tom Tuesday has an important rendezvous to keep, but he's going blind from a gunshot wound so he kidnaps Duke to act as a guide.

Tom (Brian Keith).

#218. Heather and Hamish
Written & Directed by: Allen Miner

Scotsman Samuel McIntosh wants to marry off his daughter Heather to farmer Hamish Browne, sight unseen. Once Hamish agrees, McIntosh makes him sign a contract to insure the deal.

Heather (Ann Helm), *Hamish* (Michael Parks), *Samuel McIntosh* (Liam Redmond), *Sara McIntosh* (Meg Wyllie).

#219. The Blane Wessels Story
Written by: John McGreevey

Enroute to the wagon train Blane Wessels saves Duke Shannon and three women he's escorting from a Native American attack, but the Indians will be back and one lady is about to give birth.

Blane Wessels (Robert Colbert), *Laura* (Lory Patrick), *Minna* (Virginia Christine), *Essie* (Juanita Moore).

#220. The Tom O'Neal Story
Written by: John Kneubuhl

Two young passengers on the wagon train fall in love, and when their parents object, they decide to run away and get married.

Tom O'Neal (Peter Helm), *Ellen Howard* (Brenda Scott), *Mr. O'Neal* (Myron Healey), *Mr. Howard* (Les Tremayne), *Mrs. O'Neal* (Aline Towne).

#221. The Clarence Mullins Story
Written by: Norman Jolley

Duke and Charlie enter dangerous Indian country in an attempt to locate their old friend Clarence Mullins, a minister who was ousted from the Army because he refused to fight Native Americans, and who is now preaching among them.

Clarence Mullins (Clu Gulager), *Maj. Gaston* (Carleton Young), *Harvey Mullins* (I. Stanford Jolley), *Barker* (Jim McMullan), *Esther* (Lisa Seagram).

#222. The David Garner Story
Written by: Norman Jolley

Young David Garner is determined to steal a strongbox of cash entrusted to Chris Hale, despite the objections of his girlfriend.

David (Randy Boone), *Susan* (Susan Silo), *Vern Orton* (Harry Harvey), *Judd* (Peter Whitney).

#223. Alias Bill Hawks
Written by: Norman Jolley

Bill Hawks rides into a prairie town to see an old Indian friend, and finds unfriendly people drilling for water on his friend's property who refuse to give Hawks any information about his whereabouts.

Karen Wells (Joan Freeman), *Alice Wells* (Jeanne Ball), *Martin Wells* (Arthur Space), *Burke Clayton* (Ed Nelson), *Lester Cole* (Hal Baylor), *Chester Cole* (Cliff Osmond).

#224. The Antone Rose Story
Written & Directed by: Allen Miner

Henry Ludlow, an invalid cattle rancher, sells his land and joins the wagon train to prevent his daughter Judy from marrying sheepherder Antone Rose.

Antone Rose (Charles Robinson), *Judy Ludlow* (Judi Meredith), *Henry Ludlow* (Trevor Bardette), *Nico* (Charles Herbert).

#225. The Jim Whitlow Story
Written by: Steven Ritch

Years have passed since Duke gave friend Jim Whitlow half interest in his ranch. Now the rancher has become an empire and Duke is disturbed by the way Whitlow has expanded their property.

Jim (John Kerr), *Margaret* (Ellen MacRae), *Hubbie* (Jim Davis).

#226. The Barnaby West Story
Written by: Norman Jolley

Bill Hawks befriends Barnaby West, a thirteen year old boy, who has come west alone to find his father.

Barnaby (Michael Burns), *West* (Stuart Erwin), *Karl Roberts* (Brad Morrow), *Palmer* (Dennis McCarthy).

WAGON TRAIN
Season Seven: 1963-1964
(90-Minute Episodes Filmed in Color)

	Episode Titles	Air Dates
227.	The Molly Kincaid Story	9/16/03
228.	The Fort Pierce Story	9/23/63
229.	The Gus Morgan Story	9/30/63
230.	The Widow O'Rourke Story	10/7/63
231.	The Robert Harrison Clarke Story	10/14/63
232.	The Myra Marshall Story	10/21/63
233.	The Sam Spicer Story	10/28/63
234.	The Sam Pulaski Story	11/4/63
235.	The Eli Bancroft Story	11/11/63
236.	The Kitty Pryer Story	11/18/63
237.	The Sandra Cummings Story	12/2/63
238.	The Bleeker Story	12/9/63
239.	The Story of Cain	12/16/63
240.	The Cassie Vance Story	12/23/63
241.	The Fenton Canaby Story	12/30/63
242.	The Michael Malone Story	1/6/64
243.	The Jed Whitmore Story	1/13/64
244.	The Geneva Balfour Story	1/20/64
245.	The Kat Crawley Story	1/27/64
246.	The Grover Allen Story	2/3/64
247.	The Andrew Elliott Story	2/10/64
248.	The Melanie Craig Story	2/17/64
249.	The Pearlie Garnet Story	2/24/64
250.	The Trace McCloud Story	3/2/64
251.	The Duncan McIvor Story	3/9/64

Episode Titles	Air Dates
252. The Ben Engel Story	3/16/64
253. The Whipping	3/23/64
254. The Santiago Quesada Story	3/30/64
255. The Stark Bluff Story	4/6/64
256. The Link Cheney Story	4/13/64
257. The Zebedee Titus Story	4/20/64
258. Last Circle Up	4/27/64

#227. The Molly Kincaid Story
Written by: Gene L. Coon
Directed by: Virgil Vogel

Freight line operator Kate Crawley befriends Molly Kincaid and Rome Wilson who, unknown to her, seek vengeance on the man whose cowardice resulted in their capture by the Indians.

Kate Crawley (Barbara Stanwyck), *Molly Kincaid* (Carolyn Jones), *Robert Kincaid* (Ray Danton), *Rome Wilson* (Fabian), *Martha Kincaid* (Brenda Scott), *Hankins* (Harry Carey, Jr.), *Wells* (Richard Reeves), *Merrybelle* (Pamela Austin).

#228. The Fort Pierce Story
Written by: John McGreevey
Directed by: William Witney

The wagon train heads into Indian country and Hale asks Col. Lathrop for an escort. Lathrop declines but provides a new passenger for Hale: the wife of Captain Winters who has created disturbances at the fort and has been ordered to leave.

Captain Winters (Ronald Reagan), *Mrs. Winters* (Ann Blyth), *Col. Lathrop* (John Doucette), *Beth* (Kathie Browne), *Gil* (Ron Hayes), *Sgt.* (Robert J. Wilkie).

#229. The Gus Morgan Story
Written by: Norman Jolley
Directed by: Virgil Vogel

Chris Hale agrees to accompany tycoon Gus Morgan and his brother Ethan to help them find the best route for their railroad through a snowy mountain range. Enroute disaster strikes the three.

Gus Morgan (Peter Falk), *Ethan Morgan* (Tommy Sands), *Jess* (Ken Mayer), *Ben* (Harry Swoger), *Dr. Hayes* (Harlan Warde).

#230. The Widow O'Rourke Story
Written by: Sloan Nibley & Leonard Praskins
Directed by: Joseph Pevney

Scout Cooper Smith sets out to find Duke and Charlie Wooster who are being held prisoners by Princess Mei Ling, matriarch of a hidden Chinese empire.

(Robert Fuller appears in a dual role as *Cooper Smith* and *Terence O'Rourke*.) *Mei Ling* (Carol Lawrence), *Lin Yang* (Richard Loo), *Princess Ming Lu* (Linda Ho), *Choon Fong* (Tanigoshi), *Auctioneer* (Peter Mamakos).

#231. The Robert Harrison Clarke Story
Written by: Gene L. Coon
Directed by: William Witney

An English journalist who questions the reputed hardships and dangers of the western frontier, joins the train to get first-hand knowledge.

Robert Harrison Clarke (Michael Rennie), *Gault* (Brian Keith), *Ram Singh* (Henry Silva), *Bouchette George* (Royal Dano), *Jamie* (Randy Boone), *Warbow* (George Keymas).

#232. The Myra Marshall Story
Written by: Peter Germano
Directed by: Joseph Pevney

Grace Marshall heads west on the wagon train to take her sister away from an unhappy marriage, but finds her unwilling to leave.

Myra (Suzanne Pleshette), *Grace* (Beverly Owen), *Verne* (Charles Drake), *Colin* (Rex Reason), *Nick* (Jack Lambert), *Reno* (Hal Needham), *Philip* (Dayton Lummis).

#233. The Sam Spicer Story
Written by: Norman Jolley
Directed by: R. G. Springsteen

Outlaws Sam Spicer and Reno Sutton flee after robbing a bank and take young Barnaby West as hostage.

Spicer (Clu Gulagher), *Sutton* (Ed Begley), *Hiram* (Frank Cady).

#234. The Sam Pulaski Story
Written & Directed by: Allen Miner

Sam Pulaski, a Brooklyn hoodlum, joins the wagon train with his mother and sister Rose. Cooper Smith is attracted to Rose but remembers her brother as the leader of a gang who once robbed him.

Sam (Ross Martin), *Rose* (Annette Funicello), *Mrs. Pulaski* (Jocelyn Brando), *Jersey* (Stanley Adams), *Muscles* (Richard Bakalyan), *Pocky* (Morgan Woodward).

#235. The Eli Bancroft Story
Written by: Steven Ritch
Directed by: R. G. Springsteen

Cooper Smith and a small party of travelers are left stranded in the wilderness by outlaw Eli Bancroft and his sons.

Eli (Leif Erickson), *Seth Bancroft* (Bruce Dern), *Adam Bancroft* (Carl Reindel), *Mason* (David Carradine), *Talley* (Parley Baer), *Emily* (Rachel Ames), *Jackson* (Larry J. Blake), *Noah Bancroft* (Randy Boone).

#236. The Kitty Pryer Story
Written & Directed by: Allen Miner

Kitty Pryer is about to marry Victor Harper when she discovers he is already married to someone else. When Harper is found dead, Kitty is convicted of his murder.

Kitty (Diane Hyland), *Myles Brisbane* (Bradford Dillman), *Martha Harper* (Jeanne Cooper), *Victor Harper* (Don Durant).

#237. The Sandra Cummings Story
Written by: Norman Jolley
Directed by: Virgil Vogel

Singer Sandra Cummings objects to Cooper romancing her daughter Paula. She doesn't want to see her get hurt, but Cooper is unrelenting. It seems he plans to deliberately use Paula to get back at her mother for reasons unknown.

Sandra (Rhonda Fleming), *Paula* (Cynthia Pepper), *Luke* (Michael Conrad), *Jonathan* (John Archer).

#238. The Bleeker Story
Written by: Ted Sherdeman & Jane Klove
Directed by: William Witney

Ma Bleeker and her gang, posing as farmers, join the wagon train near Fort Bridger where the army has a large supply of gold.

Ma (Joan Blondell), *Jenny* (Ruta Lee), *Al Bleeker* (Ed Nelson), *Holly Bleeker* (Holly McIntire), *Dave Bleeker* (Tim McIntire), *Bessie* (Brooke Bundy), *McFerran* (Tudor Owen), *Col. Webster* (Tyler McVey).

#239. The Story of Cain
Written & Directed by: Allen Miner

Cooper finds prospector John Cain half-dead in the desert. Once he recovers enough, he begins selling shares in his gold mine to the wagon train members. However, he later changes his mind which doesn't sit well with the travelers.

John Cain (Ron Hayes), *Ruth* (Ann Helm), *Benny* (Allen Joseph), *Sheriff* (Lane Bradford), *Doctor* (Frank Overton).

#240. The Cassie Vance Story
Written by: Betty Andrews
Directed by: Joseph Pevney

Traveler Cassie Vance is a happily married woman with a hidden past. She once did time in prison and has never told her family. When a theft occurs on the train, Cassie is accused and reveals her past to husband Adam who is unforgiving.

Cassie (Laraine Day), *Adam* (Richard Carlson), *Davie* (Kevin Corcoran), *Floyd* (Robert Strauss), *Milly* (Beverly Washburn), *Jenkins* (John Harmon), *Mrs. Jenkins* (Adrienne Marden), *Mrs. Sharp* (Eve McVeagh).

#241. The Fenton Canaby Story
Written by: Thomas Thompson
Directed by: Joseph Pevney

Chris Hale takes in Fenton Canaby, a former wagonmaster accused of deserting his wagon train, and leaving his passengers to die from thirst and starvation. Once Hale learns his true identity, the wagon train crew attempts to keep it secret from the travelers for fear of reprisal.

Fenton Canaby (Jack Kelly), *Lucy* (Barbara Bain), *Grace Lowe* (Virginia Gregg), *Byron Lowe* (Robert Cornthwaite), *Clayton* (John Hoyt), *Briggs* (I. Stanford Jolley), *Mr. Haley* (Byron Morrow), *Max* (Burt Mustin), *Simms* (Walter Reed).

#242. The Michael Malone Story
Teleplay by: Gerry Day
Story by: Gerry Day & David Richards
Directed by: Virgil Vogel

Judi Holland falls in love with wagon driver Michael Malone, unaware that he is a former priest with a troubled past.

Michael (Michael Parks), *Judi* (Joyce Bullifant), *Beth* (Judi Meredith), *Ben* (Dick York), *Paul* (Chuck Courtney).

#243. The Jed Whitmore Story
Written by: Teddi Sherman
Directed by: Virgil Vogel

Ex-convict Harry Whitmore has a story for newspaperman William Carr. Harry claims that Sheriff Frank Lewis is really his brother Jed Whitmore, a wanted outlaw.

Frank Lewis (Neville Brand), *Harry* (Karl Swenson), *Jennings* (William Mims), *Jean Lewis* (Jan Clayton), *Patsy Lewis* (Lois Roberts), *William Carr* (Les Tremayne).

#244. The Geneva Balfour Story
Written by: Ken Trevey
Directed by: Sutton Roley

A young expectant mother destroys the food supplies in an attempt to force the wagon train to return to safety.

Geneva Balfour (Sherry Jackson), *Judge Arthur Forbes* (Robert Lansing), *Aaron Balfour* (Peter Brown), *Ishmael* (Archie Moore), *Lew Pumfret* (James Griffith), *Clara Pumfret* (Kathleen Freeman), *Simon Turpin* (E. J. Andre).

#245. The Kate Crawley Story
Written by: Norman Jolley
Directed by: Virgil Vogel

A romance develops between Chris Hale and strong-willed, rough-mannered, independent Kate Crawley.

Kate (Barbara Stanwyck), *Stump Beasley* (Noah Berry, Jr.), *Pop Harmon* (Richard Reeves), *Emma* (Juney Ellis), *Jill* (Margaret Sheridan), *Jessup Harmon* (Charles Carson), *Rev. Baily* (Bill Baldwin).

#246. The Grover Allen Story
Written by: Jack Curtis
Directed by: Joseph Pevney

Grover Allen kills his tyrannical employer, then joins the wagon train west with his daughter-in-law and grandson.

Grover (Burgess Meredith), *Delia* (Nancy Gates), *Will* (Marshall Thompson), *Mr. Duskins* (Byron Foulger), *Jeff* (Scott Lane), *Phoebe* (Lillian Bronson).

#247. The Andrew Elliott Story
Written by: John Kneubuhl
Directed by: Herschel Daugherty

The U.S. Army holds Duke for questioning in the possible murder of a senator's son.

Senator Elliott (Everett Sloane), *Andrew Elliott* (Dick Sargent), *Major Ogden* (Alfred Ryder), *George* (Skip Homier), *Robert Rollins* (Myron Healey), *Nora* (Grace Lee Whitney).

#248. The Melanie Craig Story
Written by: John McGreevey
Directed by: Joseph Pevney

Duke Shannon competes with three other men for the attentions of widow Melanie Craig.

Melanie (Myra Fahey), *Rudd Basham* (Jim Davis), *Prentiss Dodd* (John Craig), *Quent Loomis* (Tony Young), *Sonny Wilkes* (Robert Torrey), *Mrs. Lowell* (Amzie Strickland), *Matt Basham* (Bobby Diamond).

#249. The Pearlie Garnet Story
Written by: Leonard Praskins
Directed by: Herschel Daugherty

Charlie Wooster suspects that pretty, young Pearlie Garnet is the thief who has been stealing supplies and looting money from the other wagons.

Pearlie (Sharon Farrell), *Duchess* (Marilyn Maxwell), *Jed Halleck* (Hugh Beaumont), *Clay Boudreau* (H.M. Wynant), *Lovey* (Aline Towne), *Sheriff* (Lane Chandler), *Ed Norton* (Ken Mayer).

#250. The Trace McCloud Story
Written by: John McGreevey
Directed by: Virgil Vogel

When a number of unsolved murders occur in the town of Bedrock, some of the townspeople decide to join the train, including the murderer.

Trace McCloud (Larry Pennell), *Lola Medina* (Audrey Dalton), *Florence Yeager* (Rachel Ames), *Ernie Weaver* (John Lupton), *Mayor Ives* (Harry Harvey, Sr.), *Ben Tatum* (Paul Newlan), *Hilda Bannister* (Nora Marlowe), *Venner* (Richard Cutting).

#251. The Duncan McIvor Story
Written by: Norman Jolley
Directed by: Herschel Daugherty

Duke Shannon and Bill Hawks are saved from hostile Indians by Lt. Duncan McIvor, an Army officer who is investigating recent thefts of military property.

Lt. McIvor (Ron Hayes), *2nd Lt. Carter* (Chris Robinson), *Mrs. Carter* (Joanna Moore), *Col. Lipton* (John Larkin), *Sgt. Jake Orly* (Gene Evans), *Pvt. James Jones* (L. Q. Jones), *Garrett* (James Griffith), *Cpl. Moller* (Mike Mazurki).

#252. The Ben Engel Story
Written by: Betty Andrews
Directed by: Joseph Pevney

Ruthless Harry Diel is saved from hanging by Ben Engel, a kindly man who Harry once tried to rob.

Ben (John Doucette), *Harry* (Clu Gulagher), *Evie Diel* (Katherine Crawford), *McCloud* (Whit Bissell), *Colin Dunn* (J. Pat O'Malley), *Matt Wilson* (Elisha Cook, Jr.), *Judge Larkin* (Frank Ferguson), *Benjie Diel* (Darby Hinton).

#253. The Whipping
Written by: Leonard Praskins
Directed by: Virgil Vogel

Bill Hawks, upset by Barnaby's recent behavior, threatens to give the youth a whipping, which leads to unexpected consequences for both of them.

March Jones (Martin Balsam), *Molly Garland* (Jeanne Cooper), *Finley* (William Fawcett), *Dr. Burke* (John Litel).

#254. The Santiago Quesada Story
Written by: Gerry Day
Directed by: Virgil Vogel

Indian Lance Starbuck is in love with Kim Case whose uncle nurses a hate for all Indians.

Lance (Perry Lopez), *James Case* (Joseph Wiseman), *Kim Case* (Jena Engstrom), *Major Starbuck* (Ed Binns), *Meachum* (Walter Coy), *Stitch* (George Keymas), *Jute* (Morgan Woodward).

#255. The Stark Bluff Story
Written & Directed by: Allen Miner

In the town of Start Bluff to pick up mail, Duke learns that his friend died in a fire and that the man's widow now works for a ruthless saloon owner.

Zeb Stark (Ray Danton), *Suzy Dufree* (Jean Hale), *Sheriff Pincus* (Peter Whitney), *Judge Pike* (Stanley Adams), *Jefferson Washington Freeman* (Hari Rhodes).

#256. The Link Cheney Story
Written by: John McGreevey
Directed by: Joseph Pevney

Gambler Euchre Jones joins the wagon train and encounters a variety of personalities attached to gambling, including his former protegé which is not a happy reunion.

Link Cheney (Charles Drake), *Ellie Riggs* (Yvonne Craig), *Tim Riggs* (Tom Simcox), *Dorothy Guilford* (Pippa Scott), *Henry Baffle* (Harry Von Zell), *Euchre Jones* (Will Kuluva).

#257. The Zebedee Titus Story
Written by: Norman Jolley
Directed by: Virgil Vogel

Chris Hale hires elderly frontier scout Zebedee Titus because of his prestigious background; then Titus is deemed responsible for Cooper's capture by Native Americans.

Titus (Neville Brand), *Maria* (Angela Dorian), *Pietro* (Robert Stanton), *Parsons* (Harry Harvey), *Maj. Hanley* (Sid Clute), *Indian Chief* (Eddie Little Sky).

#258. The Last Circle Up
Written & Directed by: Allen Miner

As the wagon train nears the end of the trail, things get heated as Hale pays off his men who immediately engage in some offbeat gambling contests for huge sums of money.

Samuel Moses (Joe De Santis), *Dewey Jameson* (Tim McIntire), *Dewhirst Jameson* (Arthur Space), *Harris Browne* (Tom Skerritt), *Hannah Moses* (Naomi Stevens), *Earl Calkins* (J. Pat O'Malley).

WAGON TRAIN
Season Eight: 1964-1965

Episode Titles	Air Dates
259. The Bob Stuart Story	9/20/64
260. The Hide Hunters	9/27/64
261. The John Gillman Story	10/4/64
262. The Race Town Story	10/11/64
263. The Barbara Lindquist Story	10/18/64
264. The Brian Conlin Story	10/25/64
265. The Alice Whitetree Story	11/1/64
266. Those Who Stay Behind	11/8/64
267. The Nancy Styles Story	11/22/64
268. The Richard Bloodgood Story	11/29/64
269. The Clay Shelby Story	12/6/64
270. Little Girl Lost	12/13/64
271. The Story of Hector Heatherington	12/20/64
272. The Echo Pass Story	1/3/65
273. The Chottsie Gubenheimer Story	1/10/65
274. The Wanda Snow Story	1/17/65
275. The Isaiah Quickfox Story	1/31/65
276. Herman	2/14/65
277. The Bonnie Brooke Story	2/21/65
278. The Miss Mary Lee McIntosh Story	2/28/65
279. The Captain Sam Story	3/21/65
280. The Betsy Blee Smith Story	3/28/65
281. The Katy Piper Story	4/11/65
282. The Indian Girl Story	4/18/65
283. The Silver Lady	4/25/65
284. The Jarbo Pierce Story	5/2/65

#259. The Bob Stuart Story
Written by: Calvin Clements
Directed by: Virgil Vogel

Ex-lawman Bob Stuart gets into a fight with an old enemy on his wedding day.

Bob Stuart (Robert Ryan), *Janice Stuart* (Vera Miles), *Keith Lance* (Tommy Sands), *Felix Colton* (Andrew Prine), *Thomas Lance* (William Smith), *Sheriff* (Stacy Harris).

#260. The Hide Hunters
Written by: John McGreevey
Directed by: Virgil Vogel

Cooper Smith and Barnaby West accompany a group of hide hunters in an effort to hunt buffalo. Unfortunately, one of them delights in taunting Barnaby.

Gib Ryker (Chris Robinson), *Zach Ryker* (Morgan Woodward), *Samantha* (Charla Doherty), *Cougar* (Ted White).

#261. The John Gillman Story
Written by: Calvin Clements
Directed by: Joseph Pevney

John Gillman is an embittered outlaw without any friends, until he meets a little orphan girl named Abigail.

John (Bobby Darin), *Abigail* (Betsy Hale), *Moore* (Whit Bissell), *Miss Roberts* (Virginia Gregg), *Gorman* (James McCallion).

#262. The Race Town Story
Written by: Calvin Clements
Directed by: Joseph Pevney

Bill Hawks and Barnaby West escort Annabelle to Sam Race's tent city of honky-tonks and con games where Annabelle learns she was hired as a saloon girl, not as an entertainer.

Sam Race (Dan Duryea), Annabelle (Cheryl Holdridge), Julie (Allyson Ames), Digger (Hal Needham).

#263. The Barbara Lindquist Story
Written by: Meyer Dolinsky
Directed by: R.G. Springsteen

Cooper Smith comes to the aid of a stagecoach being attacked by bandits, and finds the sole survivor is Bostonian Barbara Lindquist.

Barbara (Dana Wynter), *Frazer* (Barry Atwater).

#264. The Brian Conlin Story
Written by: Frank Chase
Directed by: Virgil Vogel

Immigrant Irishman Brian Conlin stumbles into the wagon train camp delirious and dust-covered. He's been continually victimized, and therefore distrustful of Hale and the passengers.

Brian Conlin (Leslie Nielsen), *Dana Barron* (Audrey Dalton), *Sean Barron* (Paul Fix), *Sara* (Eileen Baral), *Michael* (Dick Miller).

#265. The Alice Whitetree Story
Written by: John Kneubuhl

Cooper becomes involved with a half-breed Indian girl he found wandering in the wilderness.

Alice Whitetree (Diane Baker), *Morton* (Ken Lynch), *Tom Vincent* (Chuck Courtney), *Reed* (John Hoyt).

#266. Those Who Stay Behind
Written by: John McGreevey
Directed by: Virgil Vogel

Chris Hale has no room for a group of travelers wanting to join the train. Among them is ex-convict Ben Campbell whose life has been threatened by his former partner in crime.

> *Leonora Parkman* (Lola Albright), *Jud Fisher* (Bruce Dern), *Ben Campbell* (Peter Brown), *Tom Blake* (Jay North), *Danny Blake* (Dennis Holmes), *Ord Whaley* (Walter Coy).

#267. The Nancy Styles Story
Written by: Norman Jolley
Directed by: Joseph Pevney

Young and wealthy Nancy Styles is determined to reach Denver, despite Hale's edict that the wagon train will by-pass the city.

> *Nancy* (Deborah Walley), *Paul Phillips* (Ryan O'Neal), *Phineas* (James Griffith), *Homer* (Rex Reason), *Telegraph Operator* (Olan Soule).

#268. The Richard Bloodgood Story
Written by: Leonard Praskins
Directed by: Joseph Pevney

Cooper's boyhood blood brother Richard Bloodgood, now blind, joins the wagon train to kill Cooper.

> *Richard* (Guy Stockwell), *Tenny* (Reta Shaw), *Espada* (William Smith), *Young Cooper* (David Foley), *Young Richard* (Johnny Tuohy), *Guitarist* (Glenn Yarbrough).

#269. The Clay Shelby Story
Written by: Peter Germano
Directed by: R.G. Springsteen

The wagon train is in peril. Hawks is ill, Cooper's been wounded and a band of hostile Native Americans prepare to attack.

Lt. Burns (Richard Carlson), *Ann Shelby* (Celia Kaye), *Clay Shelby* (Dwayne Hickman), *Sgt. Bragan* (Mort Mills), *Cpl. Reese* (Berkeley Harris), *Mrs. Mahoney* (Gail Bonney).

#270. Little Girl Lost
Written by: Leonard Praskins
Directed by: Virgil Vogel

Charlie Wooster is the only one who catches a glimpse of a little girl before she vanishes in the night.

Robin (Eileen Baral), *Boone* (John Doucette), *Dixon* (Richard Cutting).

#271. The Story of Hector Heatherington
Written & Directed by: Allen Miner

Hector Heatherington is a would-be inventor who believes that man will fly someday. Charlie and Barnaby share his enthusiasm and join him in an attempt to launch a flying machine.

Hector (Tom Ewell), *Heather Heatherington* (Kim Darby), *Harriet Heatherington* (Jeanne Cooper).

#272. The Echo Pass Story
Written by: Calvin Clements
Directed by: Joseph Pevney

An outlaw gang, which includes two women, shoots Charlie, then force Cooper to guide them to water.

Lee Barton (Jack Lord), *Paul* (James Caan), *Bea* (Diane Brewster), *Vera* (Susan Seaforth).

#273. The Chottsie Gubenheimer Story
Written by: John McGreevey
Directed by: Joseph Pevney

Chris Hale breaks up a scuffle between gambler Jim Bannon and Chottsie Gubenheimer—Hale's former girlfriend.

Chottsie (Jeanette Nolan), *Jim Bannon* (Paul Stewart), *Chandler Ames* (John Doucette), *Skeeter Ames* (Buck Taylor), *Mrs. Wilson* (Gail Bonney).

#274. The Wanda Snow Story
Written by: Earl Hamner
Directed by: Joseph Pevney

Passenger Wanda Snow has a premonition that Cooper's life is in danger.

Wanda (Marta Kristen), *Dabney Pitts* (Arthur O'Connell), *Hiram Snow* (Dabbs Greer), *Jeremiah Stewart* (Donnelly Rhodes).

#275. The Isaiah Quickfox Story
Written by: John Kneubuhl
Directed by: Virgil Vogel

Cooper and Charlie ride into a town that appears deserted, and it seems that everyone left in a hurry.

(Jan Clayton), *Isaiah Quickfox* (Frank DeKova), *Eric Camden* (Andrew Prine), *Burt Enders* (John Doucette), *Kate* (Nancy Rennick).

#276. Herman
Written by: Ted Sherdeman & Jane Klove
Directed by: Joseph Pevney

Jamison Hershey has been able to pass safely through hostile territory because the Indians are in awe of his giant horse Herman, a Clydesdale that stands 19 hands high and weighs 3000 pounds.

Jamison (Charlie Ruggles), *William Temple* (Tim McIntire), *Martha Temple* (Linda Evans), *Biggers* (Lane Bradford).

#277. The Bonnie Brooke Story
Written & Directed by: Allen Miner

Expectant parents Don and Bonnie Brooke are in desperate need of money for Bonnie's medical care.

Bonnie (Katharine Ross), *Jack Evans* (Lee Phillips), *Don* (James Davidson), *Roger Cromwell* (Robert Emhardt).

#278. The Miss Mary Lee McIntosh Story
Written by: Gerry Day
Directed by: Virgil Vogel

Spinster Mary Lee McIntosh refuses to pay the wagon train fee which she considers outlandish, and decides to follow the train in her lone wagon.

Mary Lee (Bethel Leslie), *Daniel Delaney* (Jack Warden), *Efraim* (Kevin O'Neal), *Sgt. O'Rourke* (David McMahon), *Kurt* (Dennis McCarthy), *Man Who Steals Ponies* (Eddie Little Sky), *Stinky Bear* (Jack Big Head).

204 ❂ WAGON TRAIN: The Television Series

#279. The Captain Sam Story
Written by: Gerry Day
Directed by: Virgil Vogel

Captain Sam, a woman ferryboat skipper, receives a pleasant surprise from the wagon train: her sailor son Johnny and his wife Mary Anne.

Captain Sam (Cathy Lewis), *Johnny* (Robert Santon), *Mary Anne* (Leslie Perkins), *Biff* (Richard Wessel).

#280. The Betsy Blee Smith Story
Written & Directed by: Allen Miner

When Coop visits former girlfriend Eloise, he's asked to pose as husband of her twin sister Betsy.

Eloise/Betsy (Jennifer Billingsley), *Calvin* (Jody McCrea), *Buster Blee* (Peter Whitney), *Sylvia Blee* (Meg Wylie).

#281. The Katy Piper Story
Written by: Leonard Praskins & Stanley Dyrector
Directed by: Joseph Pevney

Barnaby West feels guilt-ridden after killing a masked bandit who turns out to be a boy the same age as he.

Katy Piper (Frances Reid), *Mrs. Reid* (Virginia Christine), *Judge* (Don Beddoe).

#282. The Indian Girl Story
Written by: Calvin Clements
Directed by: James H. Brown

The wagon train encounters an Indian girl in flight from her tribe for a supposed killing.

Indian (Ernest Borgnine), *Wilkins* (Bruce Dern), *Crazy Bear* (Michael Pate), *Patty McNeil* (Charla Doherty).

#283. The Silver Lady
Written by: Dick Nelson
Directed by: Andrew McLaglen

Cooper tells Bill the story of the Silver Lady, about the Earp brothers and an interesting woman who perished in the wreck of a stagecoach hauling silver.

Ann Read (Vera Miles), *Charlie* (Arthur O'Connell), *Doc Holiday* (Henry Silva), *Wyatt Earp* (Don Collier), *Virgil Earp* (Don Galloway), *Morgan Earp* (Michael Burns).

#284. The Jarbo Pierce Story
Written by: Calvin Clements
Directed by: William Witney

Charlie Wooster relives his younger years in Pierce's Bend as an employee of rugged trading post operator Jarbo Pierce.

Jarbo Pierce (Rory Calhoun), *Adam Pierce* (Tom Simcox), Deets (Arthur Hunnicutt), *Fortune* (Lee Philips), *Marie* (Angela Dorian), *Clyde* (Morgan Woodward), *Grant* (Mort Mills), *Marcus* (Bern Hoffman), *Samuel* (Stanley Adams), *Bimes* (Lane Bradford).

HARRY CAREY JR. in John Ford's *She Wore a Yellow Ribbon*.
He followed in the footsteps of his legendary father, appearing
in many films and television series including five episodes of
Wagon Train.

HOWARD CHRISTIE and son **JOHN** (at about age three) on a soundstage in the mid 1950s. Years later as a grown man with a teenage son, John would learn about the various people his father helped along the way.

HOWARD CHRISTIE in 1969 in his office at Universal Studios.

GREG PALMER made four appearances on *Wagon Train*. He began his career as a contract player at Universal International, and throughout the years appeared in many westerns as well as detective and sci-fi adventures. Inset: 1971 feature film, *Big Jake*.

DEBRA PAGET with **ELVIS PRESLEY** during filming of *Love Me Tender* in 1956. She was one of many notable actresses to guest star on *Wagon Train*. She appeared in *The Marie Dupree Story* and returned for *The Stagecoach Story*.

Academy Award winning actor ERNEST BORGNINE guest
starred in *The Willy Moran Story*, the premier episode of *Wagon
Train* in 1957, and appeared in the final episode filmed in 1965.
Inbetween, he appeared three other times in: *Around The Horn*,
The Estaban Zamora Story and *The Earl Packer Story*.

WARREN STEVENS began his career on Broadway and subsequently signed with 20th Century Fox. He appeared in many films and network TV shows which included numerous westerns. He guest starred on *Wagon Train* in *The Kate Parker Story* and *The John Turnbull Story.*

The *Laramie* cast in 1959. From left to right: JOHN SMITH, ROBERT CRAWFORD JR., HOAGY CARMICHAEL and ROBERT FULLER. Shortly after the series ended its run in 1963, Fuller joined the cast of *Wagon Train*.

JOHN SMITH and ROBERT FULLER as Slim Sherman and Jess Harper in a scene from *Laramie*.

JAMES DRURY as *The Virginian* in the mid 1960s. He played the role with a unique poise and maturity for nine seasons. Prior to his success on the series, Drury appeared on *Wagon Train* in *The Bleymier Story,* then played the title role in *The Cole Crawford Story.*

PETER BROWN first gained notariety as **DEPUTY JOHNNY MCKAY** on *Lawman* co-starring John Russell and Peggy Castle. He later co-starred on *Laredo* opposite Neville Brand, William Smith and Phillip Carey. His *Wagon Train* appearances include *The Adam MacKenzie Story, The Geneva Balfour Story,* and *Those Who Stay Behind.*

WILLIAM SMITH in the mid 1960s. Prior to *Laredo*, Smith co-starred as Detective Danny Keller on the ABC television series *Asphalt Jungle* starring Jack Warden and Arch Johnson. He later portrayed James Kimo Carew on *Hawaii Five-O*. He appeared in *Wagon Train's* final season in two episodes: *The Bob Stuart Story*, and *The Richard Bloodgood Story*.

ROBERT HORTON and NEHEMIAH PERSOFF in a scene
from an episode of *A Man Called Shenandoah* entitled *The Bell*
in December of 1965. Persoff (who played the title role in the
Tiburcio Mendez Story during *Wagon Train's* fifth season) would
team with Horton again in the ABC television movie *The
Dangerous Days of Kiowa Jones*.

L. Q. JONES began his career in the early 1950s in the feature
film *Battle Cry*. A colorful performer with an inimitable style,
Jones has appeared in hundreds of films and TV shows including
four episodes of *Wagon Train*.

MORGAN WOODWARD holds the distinction of most appearances by an actor on *Wagon Train*, playing a variety of roles in twelve episodes. He also guest-starred in 19 episodes of *Gunsmoke*.

DON COLLIER (with actor **SLIM PICKENS** behind him) starred as Deputy Marshal Will Forman on NBC's *Outlaws* (1960–1962). He later appeared as Wyatt Earp in the *Wagon Train* episode: *Silver Lady*, and then costarred as Sam Butler in *The High Chaparral*, also shown on NBC from 1967–1971. From 1989–1991, he played a recurring role in *The Young Riders* which aired on ABC.

JAMES LYDON has led a varied career in films and television. After appearing on the Broadway stage, he starred in the *Henry Aldrich* films for Paramount Pictures. Lydon went on to appear in numerous films and television shows including four appearances on *Wagon Train*. He also produced feature films at Warner Bros., and helped to develop several popular network television series.

PATTY McCORMACK played the title role in *The Mary Ellen Thomas Story,* a memorable holiday episode shown during Season Two on Christmas Eve in 1958. Several years before, McCormack received critical acclaim for her portrayal in *The Bad Seed,* both on Broadway and in the feature film version.

Director JOE PEVNEY *(right)* confers with LEIF ERICKSON *(left)* on the set of *The High Chaparral* in the late 1960s. After directing 27 feature films (mostly at Universal International) Pevney began working in television in the late 1950s. One of his first TV assignments was *Wagon Train* in 1958, and he went on to direct over 25 episodes during the remainder of the series run.

GREGORY WALCOTT began working in films in the early 1950s, and enjoyed a career that spanned four decades. He appeared on *Wagon Train* in *The Riley Gratton Story* and *The Cathy Eckhart Story*. In the early 1960s he costarred in the NBC series *87th Precinct*.

BUCK TAYLOR (who appeared in *The Chottsie Gubenheimer Story* during *Wagon Train's* final season) is best remembered as **NEWLY O' BRIEN** on *Gunsmoke*. He has continued to work in films and television, and is also a well-respected western artist specializing in watercolors.

Versatile ROBERT HOY as JOE BUTLER on the set of *The High Chaparral* in the late 1960s. Since the late 1940s, he has worked as a stuntman/actor/director on numerous feature films and television shows.

DENNY MILLER in recent years. He has continued to work in televison, commercials, and has also authored two acclaimed books: *Didn't You Used to Be What's His Name* (about his many experiences in the entertainment industry) and *Toxic Waste: Get to Know Your Sweat* (concerning health and physical fitness).

AUDIENCE'S FAVORITE EPISODES

Season One
1. The Willy Moran Story
4. The Ruth Owens Story
11. The Zeke Thomas Story
15. The Cliff Grundy Story
18. The Gabe Carswell Story
22. The Bill Tawnee Story
26. A Man Called Horse
27. The Sarah Drummond Story
31. The Major Adams Story—*Part Two*
28. The Monty Britton Story

Season Two
41. The Juan Ortega Story
43. The Tobias Jones Story
49. The Tent City Story
54. The Flint McCullough Story
56. The Ben Courtney Story
59. The Old Man Charvanaugh Story
60. The Annie Griffith Story
64. The Sister Rita Story
66. The Swift Cloud Story

72. Chuck Wooster— Wagonmaster

Season Three
78. The Stagecoach Story
85. The Felizia Kingdom Story
90. The Ruth Marshall Story
91. The Lita Foladaire Story
94. The Larry Hanify Story
96. The Benjamin Burns Story
105. The Amos Gibbon Story
106. Trail for Murder— *Part One*
107. Trail for Murder— *Part Two*
110. The Dr. Swift Cloud Story

Season Four
118. The Allison Justis Story
121. The Cathy Eckhart Story
123. The Colter Craven Story
124. The Jane Hawkins Story
126. The River Crossing
129. The Earl Packer Story
135. The Odyssey of Flint McCullough

136. The Beth Pearson Story
137. The Christopher Hale Story
144. The Duke Shannon Story

Season Five
153. The Captain Dan Brady Story
155. The Maud Frazier Story
158. The Jenna Douglas Story
163. The Traitor
166. The Hobie Redman Story
170. The Dr. Denker Story
174. The Lieutenant Burton Story
176. The Charlie Shutup Story
179. Swamp Devil
185. The Nancy Davis Story

Season Six
190. Wagon Train Mutiny
191. The Caroline Casteel Story
196. The Lisa Raincloud Story
206. The Davey Baxter Story
210. The Lily Legend Story
213. The Emmett Lawton Story
217. The Tom Tuesday Story
219. The Blane Wessels Story
223. Alias Bill Hawks
226. The Barnaby West Story

Season Seven
227. The Molly Kincaid Story
228. The Fort Pierce Story
230. The Widow O'Rourke Story
235. The Eli Bancroft Story
237. The Sandra Cummings Story
241. The Fenton Canaby Story
247. The Andrew Elliott Story
250. The Trace McCloud Story
253. The Whipping
255. The Stark Bluff Story

Season Eight
259. The Bob Stuart Story
261. The John Gillman Story
263. The Barbara Lindquist Story
265. The Alice Whitetree Story
268. The Richard Bloodgood Story
269. The Clay Shelby Story
270. Little Girl Lost
272. The Echo Pass Story
281. The Katy Piper Story
282. The Indian Girl Story

WAGON TRAIN
Production Staff
(1957-1965)

Executive Producer/Producer:
Richard Lewis (1957–1958)

Producer:
Howard Christie (1958–1965)

Associate Producers:
Boris Ingster (1957–1958)
Frederick Shorr (1958–1965)

Series Cinematography
Benjamin Kline
Bud Thackery
Walter Strenge
Herbert Kirkpatrick
John L. Russell
Lionel Lindon
Richard Rawlings
Ray Flin
Robert Tobey
John F. Warren

Series Film Editing
Tony Martinelli
Gene Palmer
Buddy Small
Lee Huntington
Robert Seiter

Edward Biery
Marston Fay
Sam E. Waxman

Assistant Directors
Abby Singer
James H. Brown
Charles S. Gould
Ben Bishop (Unit Manager)
George Lollier
    (Unit Manager)
Lester William Berke
Edward K. Dodds
Henry Kline
Carter DeHaven III
Chuck Colean
Ray Taylor, Jr.
Norman Cook
Jack Doran
Frank Losee
John Clarke Bowman
Donald Baer
Lou Watt

Sound Department
Melvin Metcalfe, Sr.
David H. Moriarty

Sound Department *(con't.)*
Corson Jowett
William Lynch
Jim Bullock

Art Directors
Howard E. Johnson
John L. Lloyd
Russell Kimball

Set Decoration
Ralph Sylos
John McCarthy, Jr.
Perry Murdock
Clarence Steensen

Music Department
Stanley Wilson
    (Music Supervisor)
Jerome Moross *(Composer:*
    Theme Music)
Sammy Fain *(Composer:*
    Theme Music)
Jack Brooks *(Composer:*
    Theme Music)
Henri Rene *(Composer:*
    Theme Music)
Bob Russell *(Composer:*
    Theme Music)
Lloyd Apperson *(Composer:*
    Additional Music)
Herman Stein *(Music Cues)*
Sidney Fine *(Original Music)*
Morton Stevens *(Original*
    Music)
Cyril J. Mockridge *(Original*
    Music)

Makeup Department
Florence Bush
Jack Baron
Larry Germain
Bud Westmore
Robert Dawn
Leo Lotito, Jr.

Costume and Wardrobe
Vincent Dee *(Costume*
    Supervisor)
Burton Miller *(Costume*
    Design)

**Camera and Electric
Department**
Eric C. Williman *(Lamp*
    Operator)

Stunts
Jesse Wayne
Dean Smith

Editorial Department
David J. O'Connell
Robert Brower
Richard G. Wray
George Fredrick

Assistant to Producer
Robert Eggenweiler

WAGON TRAIN
Theme Music

THERE WERE several *Wagon Train* themes during the course of the series run. The first season theme *"Wagon Train"* was an instrumental written by Henri Rene and Bob Russell. In the second year, a more modern sounding theme was introduced. It was called *"(Roll Along) Wagon Train"* and was written by Sammy Fain and Jack Brooks. The song was sung by Johnny O'Neill. Midway through the second season, this was replaced by an instrumental version by Stanley Wilson.

In the third season a more traditional-sounding score was used entitled *"Wagons Ho!"* This theme (written and conducted by Jerome Moross) was used for the remainder of the series run. It was rerecorded by Stanley Wilson for the last two seasons.

BIOGRAPHIES

WARD BOND

While playing college football at USC, Ward Bond was introduced to director John Ford by his friend and roommate Marion Morrison (who later became John Wayne). He would appear in 26 films directed by Ford.

From the early 1930s through the mid-1950s, Bond was one of the busiest character actors in Hollywood, playing a variety of supporting roles in a number of memorable movies.

In 1957, Bond was cast as Wagonmaster Seth Adams on the NBC television series *Wagon Train*, and he became a huge TV star. He died suddenly from a heart attack in November of 1960, during the fourth season of the series. A partial list of his many films include *Rio Bravo, The Searchers, Mister Roberts, The Long Gray Line, The Bob Mathias Story, Johnny Guitar, Hondo, The Quiet Man, Operation Pacific, Wagonmaster, 3 Godfathers, Joan of Arc, The Time of Your Life, Fort Apache, My Darling Clementine, The Fugitive, Unconquered, It's a Wonderful Life, They Were Expendable, A Guy Named Joe, Gentleman Jim, The Maltese Falcon, The Shepherd of the Hills, Sergeant York, Tobacco Road, The Long Voyage Home, City for Conquest, Kit Carson, The Mortal Storm, Virginia City, The Grapes of Wrath, Gone with Wind, Drums Along the Mohawk, Young Mr. Lincoln, Union Pacific, Dodge City, The Oklahoma Kid, Made for Each Other, They Made Me a Criminal, Son of Frankenstein, You Can't Take It with You, Dead End,* and *It Happened One Night.*

His TV appearances include *General Electric Theater, Cavalcade of America, Schlitz Playhouse of Stars, Climax, Ford Television Theatre,* and *Suspense.*

ERNEST BORGNINE

Ernest Borgnine began his career with the Barter Theatre in Abingdon, Virginia, playing a variety of roles over a four year period. In 1949, he made his Broadway debut in *Harvey.* In the early 1950s, Borgnine moved to Hollywood to pursue a career in movies. His memorable performance as Sgt. Fatso Judson, a menacing stockade supervisor in *From Here to Eternity* brought acclaim and many subsequent film roles as a "heavy." However, Borgnine displayed another facet of his acting personality as Marty Piletti, a lonely and sensitive butcher in *Marty*, which won him an Academy Award for Best Actor. His performance as Tom Hurley opposite Bette Davis in *The Catered Affair* was equally affecting.

Borgnine's long-lasting career includes over a hundred feature films, three television series, and many guest star appearances on TV. His film work includes *The Stranger Wore a Gun, Johnny Guitar, Demetrius and the Gladiators, The Bounty Hunter, Vera Cruz, Run for Cover, Violent Saturday, The Last Command, Jubal, The Best Things in Life Are Free, Three Brave Men, The Vikings, The Badlanders, Torpedo Run, Summer of the Seventeenth Doll, The Rabbit Trap, Pay or Die, Barabbas, The Flight of the Phoenix, The Oscar, Chuka, The Dirty Dozen, The Legend of Lylah Clare, Ice Station Zebra, The Split, The Wild Bunch, Willard, Hannie Caulder, The Neptune Factor, Emperor of the North Pole, The Poseidon Adventure, The Devil's Rain, Hustle, Shoot, The Greatest, The Black Hole, When Time Ran Out, Deadly Blessing, Escape from New York, Abilene, Hoover, The Long Ride Home, Oliviero Rising, Strange Wilderness*, and *Aces 'N Eights.*

Some of his many television credits include: *The Blue Light, The District, Family Law, 7th Heaven, Touched by an Angel, Walker, Texas Ranger, Early Edition, JAG,, The Single Guy, The Commish, Jake and the Fatman, The Dirty Dozen: The Deadly Mission, Murder She Wrote, Airwolf (as Dominic Santini), The Dirty Dozen: The Next Mission, Alice in Wonderland, Matt Houston, Magnum P.I., The Love Boat, All Quiet on the Western Front, The Ghost of Flight 401, Jesus of Nazareth, Little House on the Prairie, Get Smart, Run for Your Life, Bob Hope Presents The Chrysler Theater, McHale's Navy (As Lt. Cmdr. Quinton McHale), General Electric Theater, Alcoa Premiere, Laramie, Zane Grey Theater, Wagon Train, Navy Log*, and *Make Room for Daddy.*

JAMES H. BROWN

James Brown began his career at Revue Studios. In 1955 he became a second assistant director. Two years later, Brown began a lengthy career as a first assistant, unit manager, director and producer.

His long list of diverse feature films and network television shows includes Alfred Hitchcock's *The Birds* and *Marnie, Harper, Secrets (MOW), Alcatraz: The Whole Shocking Story (Miniseries), To Kill a Cop (Miniseries), Seven Brides for Seven Brothers, The Quest, Odd Couple, Wagon Train, Riverboat, Laramie*, and hundreds more.

PETER BROWN

Peter Brown first began acting while stationed on an army base in Alaska where he organized a theater group. After training in the acting program at UCLA, Brown began to find work at Warner Bros. in various television westerns. After appearing in *Colt .45, Maverick*, and *Sugarfoot*, Brown was cast as Deputy Johnny McKay on the ABC television series *Lawman*, which ran for four seasons. He later co-starred as Chad Cooper in the NBC series *Laredo* (1965–1967). Over the next four decades he has continued to appear in films and network TV shows. His film work includes *Hell to Pay, Three Bad Men, Big Chuck-Little Chuck, The Wedding Planner, Asylum, Fists of Iron, The Messenger, The Aurora Encounter, Piranha, Kitten With a Whip, Ride the Wild Surf, A Tiger Walks, Summer Magic, Merrill's Marauders, The Young Philadelphians, Onionhead, The Violent Road, Marjorie Morningstar,* and *Sayonara*.

His many television credits include *JAG, One West Waikiki, Wings, The Bold and the Beautiful* (as Blake Hayes), *Baywatch, Generations, Hunter, 1st and Ten, Aaron's Way, Ohara, One Life to Live* (as Charles Saunders III), *The A-Team, Airwolf, Simon and Simon, Riptide, The Fall Guy, Whiz Kids, Manimal, T. J. Hooker, Hart to Hart, Magnum P.I., Dallas, Fantasy Island, The Young and the Restless* (as Robert Laurence), *The Dukes of Hazzard, Project U.F.O., Salvage, The Eddie Capra Mysteries, Vegas, Charlie's Angels, Wonder Woman, Quincy M.E., The Streets of San Francisco, Days of Our Lives* (as Greg Peters), *Police Woman, Matt Helm, Marcus Welby, The Bob Newhart Show, Medical Center, Mission Impossible, Dan August, My Three Sons, The Most Deadly*

Game, The Mod Squad, The Virginian, Wagon Train, Redigo, 77 Sunset Strip, Cheyenne, and *Hawaiian Eye.*

MICHAEL BURNS

After a successful acting career as a child, teen and young adult, Michael Burns left the acting profession to become a history professor at Mt. Holyoke College in New England. After twenty-two years, Burns retired from teaching, moved to Kentucky, restored a historic farm, and began to raise horses.

His television credits include *Police Woman, The Tony Randall Show, The Bionic Woman, Most Wanted, The Streets of San Francisco, Petrocelli, The Manhunter, Barnaby Jones, Love American Style, The Mod Squad, Sarge, Gidget Gets Married, Hawaii Five-O, Medical Center, The Partridge Family, The Doris Day Show, The Virginian, The F.B.I., The Andersonville Trial, Gunsmoke, Marcus Welby, Then Came Bronson, Dragnet 1967, The Outcasts, Journey to Shiloh, The Big Valley, Cowboy in Africa, Daniel Boone, Tarzan, Dundee and the Culhane, Bonanza, The Road West, The Legend of Jesse James, A Man Called Shenandoah, Lassie, Kraft Suspense Theater, Alcoa Premiere, The Twilight Zone, The Tall Man, Alfred Hitchcock Presents, General Electric Theater, Tales of Wells Fargo,* and *The Many Loves of Dobie Gillis.*

His films includes *Santee, That Cold Day in the Park, The Mad Room, The Private Navy of Sgt. O'Farrell, 40 Guns to Apache Pass, The Raiders, Mr. Hobbs Takes a Vacation,* and *The Wizard of Baghdad.*

HARRY CAREY, JR.

Harry Carey Jr. is the son of western star and character actor Harry Carey. His father nicknamed him "Dobe" because of his red hair. It reminded him, his father said, of the red Adobe soil which was so plentiful on their ranch in California.

As a young man, "Dobe" studied voice in New York. His first paying job in *Railroads on Parade* at the New York World's Fair, was not as a singer but because he could ride a horse. After working as an NBC page boy, he served three years in the Navy during World War II. While still in the service, he married Marilyn Fix, the daughter of veteran actor Paul Fix.

In 1946 he was offered a role in a B movie *Rolling Home*, and followed his father into the motion picture business. Shortly after, young Carey tested for Raoul Walsh's *Pursued* and got the part. This was followed by the Howard Hawks classic *Red River*, the first of 11 films he would make with John Wayne.

After Harry Carey, Sr. passed away in 1947, John Ford decided to do a remake of *Three Godfathers* (which he had done with Carey, Sr. in 1919). Wayne was to play Harry's role with Carey Jr. playing the "kid." He became a member of the John Ford stock company and appeared in many of the classics such as *She Wore a Yellow Ribbon, Wagonmaster, Rio Grande, The Searchers, Two Rode Together, The Long Gray Line, Mister Roberts* and *Cheyenne Autumn*.

Harry Carey, Jr. has appeared in close to 100 films as well as a few hundred TV shows. His films include *The Sunchaser, Tombstone, The Exorcist III, Back to the Future Part III, Illegally Yours, The Whales of August, Mask, Gremlins, Endangered Species, Nickelodeon, Take a Hard Ride, Cahill, U.S. Marshall, Trinity Is Still My Name, Big Jake, One More Train to Rob, Something Big, The Moonshine War, Dirty Dingus Magee, One More Time, The Undefeated, Death of a Gunfighter, Bandolero, Devil's Brigade, The Way West, The Ballad of Josie, The Rare Breed, Alvarez Kelly, Shenandoah, From Hell to Texas, The River's Edge, The Great Locomotive Chase, San Antone, Beyond the 12-Mile Reef,* and *Warpath*.

TV credits include *Last Stand at Saber River, Wyatt Earp: Return to Tombstone, Adventures of William Tell, Princess Daisy, The Shadow Riders, B. J. Stryker, Knight Rider, CHIPs, Little House on the Prairie, Gunsmoke, Doc Elliot, Banacek, The Virginian, Mannix, The Outcasts, Cimarron Strip, Bonanza, The Rounders, The Legend of Jesse James, Branded, Redigo, Wagon Train, Stoney Burke, Checkmate, Frontier Circus, Rawhide, Perry Mason, The Rifleman, Whispering Smith, Laramie, The Tall Man, Overland Trail, Have Gun Will Travel, Broken Arrow,* and *Tombstone Territory*.

DON COLLIER

Don Collier began his career in western films such as *Fort Apache* and *Davy Crockett, Indian Scout*.

In 1960 he starred as U.S. Deputy Marshall Will Foreman in the NBC series Outlaws. In the late 1960s he co-starred as Sam Butler in NBC's *The High Chaparral* which ran for four seasons. Collier also played the recurring role of William Tompkins in *The Young Riders*, an ABC TV series that ran from 1989–1992. His many television guest appearances include *Vanishing Point, Legend, Bonanza: Under Attack, Gunsmoke: One Man's Justice, Telling Secrets, Gunsmoke: To the Last Man, El Diablo, War and Remembrance, Once Upon a Texas Train, Highway to Heaven, Little House on the Prairie, Winds of War, The Last Ride of the Dalton Gang, The Sacketts, Mr. Horn, How the West Was Won, Aspen, The Waltons, Land of the Giants, Bonanza, Death Valley Days, Branded, Wagon Train, The Virginian, Profiles in Courage, Perry Mason, Temple Houston* and *The Wide Country*.

Film work includes *Tombstone, Benefit of the Doubt, Kid, The Cellar, Flip, The Undefeated, 5 Card Stud, The War Wagon, El Dorado, Incident at Phantom Hill, Safe at Home, Seven Ways from Sundown*, and *Twelve Hours to Kill*.

JAMES DRURY

After appearing in numerous films and episodic television series from the mid-1950s, James Drury was cast in the title role of *The Virginian* which debuted on NBC in the fall of 1962. Ironically, he had first played the part in a summer series of anthology dramas called *Decision* in 1958.

Several years after the series ended its lengthy run, Drury starred in another TV series, *Firehouse*, in the mid-1970s. In the 1990s he played the recurring role of Captain Tom Price in *Walker, Texas Rangers*. In 1991, Drury was inducted into the Hall of Great Western Performers at the National Cowboy and Western Heritage Museum in Oklahoma.

His film work includes *Hell to Pay, Maverick, The Young Warriors, Ride the High Country, Third of a Man, Ten Who Dared, Pollyanna, Toby Tyler, Good Day for a Hanging, Bernadine, Love Me Tender, The Last Wagon, Forbidden Planet, The Tender Trap*, and *Love Me or Leave Me*.

His many TV credits include: *Kung Fu: The Legend Continues, The Adventures of Briscoe County Jr., The Gambler Returns: The Luck of the Draw, The Fall Guy, Alias Smith and Jones, The Devil and Miss Sarah, Breakout, It Takes a Thief, Wagon Train, The Detectives Starring Robert Taylor, Perry Mason, Rawhide, Michael Shayne, The Loretta Young Show, Gunsmoke, The Rebel, Lock Up, Men into Space, Cheyenne, Black*

Saddle, Lawman, Bronco, Richard Diamond, Private Detective, Trackdown, Have Gun Will Travel, Zane Grey Theater, Broken Arrow, and *Alfred Hitchcock Presents.*

RHONDA FLEMING

Known to many as one of the more beautiful and glamorous women in Hollywood, Rhonda Fleming first drew acclaim for her portrayal of Mary Carmichael in Alfred Hitchcock's *Spellbound*. She went on to appear in such classic films as *Out of the Past, Spiral Staircase, A Connecticut Yankee in King Arthur's Court, Gunfight at the O.K. Corral,* and *Home Before Dark.*

Off-camera, Fleming has actively participated in many humanitarian organizations. Along with her late husband Ted Mann, she established the Rhonda Fleming Mann Clinic for Women's Comprehensive Care at UCLA Medical Center, as well as a second medical facility two years later. She also helped to build the Jerusalem Film Institute in Israel.

Her many film credits include *Waiting for the Wind, The Crowded Sky, The Big Circus, Alias Jesse James, Bullwhip, The Buster Keaton Story, While the City Sleeps, Slightly Scarlet, The Best of Broadway, Yankee Pasha, Inferno, Pony Express, Tropic Zone, Hong Kong, Crosswinds, Cry Danger, The Eagle and the Hawk,* and *The Great Lover.*

Television guest appearances include *The Love Boat, Ellery Queen, Kung Fu, Police Woman, McMillan and Wife, Search, The Virginian, Bob Hope Presents the Chrysler Theater, Burke's Law, Wagon Train, Follow the Sun, The Dick Powell Theater,* and *Death Valley Days.*

DIANE FOSTER

Diane Foster grew up in Edmonton, Alberta and later began her career in England. She arrived in Hollywood in the 1950s and was placed under contract to Columbia. She appeared in a number of films throughout the decade. In the 1960s she guest-starred in many episodic television shows before retiring in 1967 to donate more time to family. She later became an accomplished painter/artist.

Her feature film work includes *The Last Hurrah, Gideon's Day,*

The Deep Six, The Brothers Rico, Night Passage, Monkey on My Back, The Kentuckian, The Violent Men, The Bamboo Prison, Three Hours to Kill, Drive a Crooked Road, Three's Company, Bad for Each Other, The Steel Key, Isn't Life Wonderful, The Lost Hours, and *The Quiet Woman.*

Television credits include: *The Wild Wild West, Green Acres, The Big Valley, Perry Mason, Honey West, Ben Casey, The Fugitive, The Rogues, Petticoat Junction, My Three Sons, Breaking Point, Kraft Mystery Theater, 77 Sunset Strip, Going My Way, The Gallant Men, The Lloyd Bridges Show, The Eleventh Hour, Bus Stop, Gunsmoke, The Detectives Starring Robert Taylor, Tales of Wells Fargo, Outlaws, Checkmate, Route 66, Laramie, Have Gun Will Travel, The Roaring 20s, Peter Gunn, The Deputy, Bonanza, Bringing Up Buddy, Thriller, Bourbon Street Beat, Wagon Train, Shotgun Slade, General Electric Theater, Overland Trail, Riverboat*, and *Westinghouse Desilu Playhouse.*

ROBERT FULLER

Robert Fuller traveled an interesting road enroute to becoming a western TV star. Born in New York and raised in Key West, he eventually moved to California. Along the way he danced in the chorus line in *Gentlemen Prefer Blondes* (starring Marilyn Monroe), served in the Korean War, studied at the Neighborhood Playhouse in New York with Sandy Meisner, and was cast by William Wyler in his first role in *Friendly Persuasion* (in a scene with Gary Cooper) because of his sideburns. Over the next three years, Fuller played featured and guest star roles in a variety of TV programs which included *Wagon Train* and *Cimarron City*. Revue Studios' casting executives offered him the second lead in *Markham* (a detective series starring Ray Milland) but Fuller declined, preferring to do a western. He was then offered *Laramie* but declined again when the studio offered him the role of Slim Sherman, which he knew he was not right for, instead of the part of Jess Harper which fit him like a glove.

However, the V.P. of casting at Revue was impressed by Fuller's confidence and earnestness, and sensed the young actor knew something he didn't. Fuller was tested for Jess Harper, got the role and the series ran for four successful years. After *Laramie*, Fuller was cast as Scout Cooper Smith in *Wagon Train* for the show's final two seasons. Film roles followed including *Return of the Seven* (the sequel to *The Magnificent Seven*), and the critically acclaimed *The Hard Ride*, which led to producer Jack Webb offering Fuller a starring role in the TV series *Emergency* which ran for seven years on NBC. Fuller continued to work throughout the 1980s and 1990s in a wide variety of roles.

In 2008 Fuller received the Western Heritage Award from the National Cowboy and Western Heritage Museum in Oklahoma City. He has also won the Buffalo Bill Award for outstanding western entertainment; and in 1975 was given a star on the Hollywood Walk of Fame. Fuller's success overseas has earned him a number of prestigious awards including: The Best Actor Award in Japan; The Japanese Golden Order of Merit (awarded to him by the Empress of Japan); and the Otto Award (The German equivalent to the Emmy) which he won five times.

His film credits include *Maverick, Megaforce, Separate Ways, Gatling Gun, Return of the Seven, The Hard Ride, Incident at Phantom Hill, Teenage Thunder,* and *The Brain from Planet Arous.*

His many television appearances include: *Walker, Texas Ranger, JAG, Diagnosis Murder, Viper, Seinfeld, Renegade, Kung Fu: The Legend Continues, The Adventures of Briscoe County, Paradise, Murder She Wrote, Bonanza: The Next Generation, Tour of Duty, The Fall Guy, Matt Houston, The Love Boat, Adam-12, Hec Ramsey, Dan August, Mission Impossible, The Big Valley, The Virginian, Them Monroes, Kraft Suspense Theater, Mike Hammer, The Life and Legend of Wyatt Earp, The Restless Gun, Highway Patrol, M-Squad, The Adventures of Rin Tin Tin, Panic,* and *The Californians.*

LISA GAYE

Beautiful and talented, Lisa Gaye (the younger sister of Debra Paget) began her career as a trained dancer, and later segued into acting. Throughout the 1950s and 1960s she guest-starred on hundreds of network television shows including many of the popular western series. She retired from acting in 1970 to donate more time to family.

Her many television appearances include *The Mod Squad, The Flying Nun, Death Valley Days, I Dream of Jeannie, The Wild Wild West, Get Smart, The Time Tunnel, Hank, The Smothers Brothers Show, Burke's Law, Mister Roberts, Mona McCluskey, Bachelor Father, Bat Masterson,*

Adventures in Paradise, 77 Sunset Strip, Wagon Train, Maverick, Check-mate, Rawhide, Cheyenne, Wanted: Dead or Alive, Markham, Bourbon Street Beat, Hawaiian Eye, Going My Way, Surfside Six, Bronco, Laramie, Tales of Wells Fargo, Men Into Space, The Millionaire, Mr. Lucky, Sea Hunt, Colt-45, Tombstone Territory, Black Saddle, Have Gun–Will Travel, Zorro, Mike Hammer, The Bob Cummings Show, and *The Thin Man.*

Her films credits include *The Violent Ones, Ten Thousand Bedrooms, Shake Rattle and Roll, Rock Around the Clock, Ain't Misbehavin', Magnificent Obsession, Drums Across the River, Yankee Pasha,* and *The Glenn Miller Story.*

ROBERT HORTON

Robert Horton first appeared in Lewis Milestone's *A Walk in the Sun* while still in college. After graduating from UCLA, he studied in New York at the American Theater Wing. Upon returning to California, Horton appeared in modest-budget films for Warner Bros. and Twentieth Century Fox. After auditioning for Anthony Mann's *The Naked Spur* at M.G.M., he was placed under contract and appeared in seven films during a three year period. In 1955 Horton co-starred with Jack Kelly and Nan Leslie in *King's Row*, a Warner Bros. television series based on the 1941 feature film. After the series ended, Horton guested on several *Alfred Hitchcock Presents*, as well as *Cavalcade Theater* before winning the role of Flint McCullough in *Wagon Train*. After five years on the series, Horton left to pursue a career in the musical theater. He appeared on Broadway in *110 in the Shade* (the musical re-make of *The Rainmaker*), as well as regional theater productions of *Oklahoma, Carousel, Brigadoon, Kismet,* and *Guys and Dolls.* In the mid-60s he returned to California to star in ABC's *A Man Called Shenandoah* which ran for one season. Horton starred in several television TV movies throughout the remainder of the '60s, and over the next two decades segued between theater and occasional network TV appearances. In the early 1980s he appeared on the CBS daytime drama *As The World Turns.*

His television appearances include *Red River (MOW), Murder She Wrote, Houston Knights, The Hardy Boys, Police Woman, Longstreet, Foreign Exchange (MOW), The Spy Killer (MOW),* and *The Dangerous Days of Kiowa Jones (MOW).*

Films include *The Green Slime, The Man is Armed, Men of the Fighting Lady, Prisoner of War, Arena, The Story of Three Loves, Bright Road, Code Two, Return of the Texan, Apache War Smoke, Pony Soldier,* and *The Tanks Are Coming.*

His stage work includes such plays as *Zorba the Greek, The Music Man, The Man of La Mancha, Pajama Game, 1776, Picnic, The Rainmaker, The Hasty Heart, All My Sons, Cat on a Hot Tin Roof, Death of a Salesman, The Odd Couple, 6 Rooms Riv Vu, Same Time Next Year, There's a Girl in My Soup, I Do I Do, Catch Me If You Can, The Man,* and *Night Must Fall.*

His albums include: *Original Cast Album: 110 in the Shade, The Very Thought of You, A Man Called Shenandoah,* and *Robert Horton at the London Palladium.*

ROBERT HOY

Robert Hoy has enjoyed a lengthy and productive career as an actor, stuntman, and second unit director. He is best remembered to TV viewers as Joe Butler on *The High Chaparral* (1967–1971).

Some of his many television appearances include *JAG, Walker, Texas Ranger, Desperado, Dallas (recurring), Zorro, The Young Riders, Our House, Dirty Dozen: The Series, Magnum P.I., Crazy Like a Fox, Bonanza: The Next Generation, Fantasy Island, Six Million Dollar Man, McMillan and Wife,* and *The Rockford Files.*

His film credits include *The Legend of the Long Ranger, Bite the Bullet, The Outlaw Josey Wales, The Enforcer, Bronco Billy, Nevada Smith,* and *The Great Race.*

Hoy was also the 2nd Unit Director and Stunt Coordinator on the *Zorro* series (filmed in Spain) and on the pilot of *The Three Musketeers.* Earlier in his career, he earned a reputation as one of the top stuntmen in the film industry, and for many years, he doubled for the lead actors in numerous films such as *Spartacus, The Defiant Ones, Operation Petticoat, To Hell and Back, Saskatchewan, Drumbeat,* and *River of No Return.*

L. Q. JONES

Born Justus McQueen in the Lone Star State, he attended the University of Texas at Austin, then worked as a horse and cattle rancher in Nicaragua where he also had a dairy and a cheese factory. Upon returning to the States, friend Fess Parker suggested McQueen venture to Hollywood and audition for a Warner Bros. film he was doing called *Battle Cry*. The casting directed was not that impressed but Raoul Walsh, the director, was. He had McQueen test and picked him over 200 other actors. After completing the film, McQueen took the name of the character he played—L. Q. Jones.

Over the next fifty years, Jones would appear in a lengthy list of feature films and network television shows. He also wrote, produced and directed several movies. One of them, *A Boy and His Dog* (based on a Harlan Ellison novella) became one of the only films (aside from the Disney pictures) to achieve success on a worldwide level. In 1975, it won the Science Fiction Achievement Award for Dramatic Presentation, and also the Hugo Award. In 2000, Jones was given the Golden Boot Award for his contribution to the western film and television industry. He was also the recipient of the International Star Award in 2001.

Some of his many films include *A Prairie Home Companion, The Mark of Zorro, The Patriot, The Edge, Casino, Lone Wolf McQuade, Sacred Ground, White Line Fiver, Pat Garrett and Billy The Kid, The Ballad of Cable Hogue, The Wild Bunch, Hang 'em High, Stay Away Joe, Nevada Smith, Major Dundee, Ride the High Country, Hell Is for Heroes, Cimarron, Flaming Star, Ten Who Dared, Battle of the Coral Sea, The Young Lions, The Naked and the Dead, Buchanan Rides Alone, Men in War, Love Me Tender, Between Heaven and Hell, Toward the Unknown, Santiago, Target Zero,* and *The Annapolis Story.*

A partial list of his television work includes *Dr. Vegas, In Cold Blood, Tornado, Renegade, Walker, Texas Ranger, The A-Team, The Yellow Rose (recurring as Sheriff Lew Wallace), Matt Houston, Voyagers, The Dukes of Hazzard, Riker, Walking Tall, Charlie's Angels, The Sacketts, How the West Was Won, Columbo, Matt Helm, Kung Fu, Ironside, Manhunter, Mrs. Sundance, Alias Smith and Jones, The Bold Ones, Gunsmoke, Cades County, The F.B.I., Lancer, Hondo, Hawaii Five-O, The Big Valley, The Virginian (recurring as Belden), Cimarron Strip, Laramie, Route 66, Have Gun Will Travel, The Rifleman, Lawman, Tales of Wells Fargo, The*

Detectives Starring Robert Taylor, The Rebel, Tightrope, Johnny Ringo, Black Saddle, Annie Oakley, and *Cheyenne* (as Smitty).

JAMES LYDON

James Lydon has been an actor, writer, producer and director. He began his career on Broadway and was summoned to Hollywood where he soon after starred as *Henry Aldrich* in a series of films for Paramount. He later appeared in *Strange Interlude, Life with Father, The Time of Your Life, Joan of Arc, Tucson, The Magnificent Yankee, Oh! Susanna,* and *Island in the Sky.*

In the early 1950s Lydon appeared on *The First Hundred Years* (the first daytime drama on network TV) and co-wrote episodes with writer Jean Holloway. Over a thirty-year period, Lydon appeared in hundreds of television shows. In 1958 he began to work in production, helping to create 77 *Sunset Strip,* producing several films at Warner Bros. (with William Conrad) in the mid-60s, and contributing to the development of *MASH* in 1972.

His many network TV credits include *St. Elsewhere, Misfits of Science, Simon and Simon, The Fall Guy, Cannon, Ellery Queen, Gunsmoke, Adam-12, Police Story, Disneyland, The Jimmy Stewart Show, O'Hara U.S. Treasury, Cades County, The F.B.I., Wagon Train, Hennessey, Checkmate, The Life and Legend of Wyatt Earp, Wanted: Dead or Alive, The Untouchables, Lassie, General Electric Theater, Peter Gunn, Bronco, Tightrope, M-Squad, Man with a Camera, Maverick, Lawman,* and *The Real McCoys.*

BOYD MAGERS

Boyd Magers began his career in radio broadcasting at various stations around the country where he also served as program director. After leaving radio, he established Video West, Inc., specializing in vintage western films and TV series by mail order. At the same time he began contributing articles on western films to *Country Style* magazine. From there, he wrote regular columns in *Big Reel, Serial Report* (which he now owns and distributes to collectors), *Country and Western Variety, Under Western Skies, Film Collector's Registry, Classic Images,* and *Movie*

Collector's World. Currently, Magers publishes *Western Clippings* which is distributed to over 1,000 subscribers.

An accomplished author, his first book, *Western Women* published by McFarland in 1999, contains 50 interviews with leading ladies. A sequel, *Ladies of the Western*, was published in 2002. His subsequent books include *So You Wanna See Cowboy Stuff? (The Western Movie TV Tour Guide)*, *The Films of Audie Murphy*, *Best of the Badman*, and *Gene Autry Westerns.*

Magers has also moderated over 150 western celebrity guest star discussion panels at film festivals in Lone Pine, CA, Memphis, TN, Knoxville, TN, Charlotte, NC, Apache Junction, AZ, Sonora, AZ, Kanab, UT, and Victorville, CA.

In addition, his collection of western movie memorabilia has been on exhibit at the Herbert Hoover Presidential Library in Iowa, and the Clinton Presidential Library in Arkansas.

PATTY MCCORMACK

Audiences of every medium recognize Patty from her more than six decades of stage, screen, and television appearances. She debuted on Broadway at age six as Cathy in *Touchstone* (starring Ossie Davis). She returned to Broadway two years later as pigtailed and evil little Rhoda Penmark in *The Bad Seed*, a role she recreated in Mervyn LeRoy's classic film, winning both Academy Award and Golden Globe nominations.

Her film credits include: *Frost/Nixon*, *Heart of the Beholder*, *Shallow Ground*, *Inhabited*, *The Medicine Show*, *Choosing Mathias*, *The Kiss*, *Target*, *Mommy*, *Mommy 2: Mommy's Day*, *Saturday the 14th Strikes Back*, *Bug*, *The Mini-Skirt Mob*, *The Adventures of Huckleberry Finn*, and *Kathy 'O.*

Her television movie credits include: *Night Partners*, *Invitation to Hell*, *On Wings of Eagles*, *Silent Predators*, *Acceptable Risk*, *Mystery Woman: Snapshot*, and *Gone but Not Forgotten.*

Her many TV guest appearances include *The Sopranos*, *What About Brian*, *Grey's Anatomy*, *Shark*, *Criminal Minds*, *Cold Case*, *Entourage*, *NYPD Blue*, *Baywatch*, *Empty Nest*, *Doogie Howser*, *Murder She Wrote*, *Magnum P.I.*, *Dallas* (recurring as Evelyn Michaelson), *The Ropers* (recurring as Anne Brooks), *Remington Steele*, *Hotel*, *Fantasy Island*,

Love Boat, Barnaby Jones, The Streets of San Francisco, Wild Wild West, Peck's Bad Girl (Series Lead), *Wagon Train, Route 66, Rawhide, and Playhouse 90* (originating the role of Helen Keller in *The Miracle Worker*).

FRANK MCGRATH

Frank McGrath began his career as a stuntman in movies in the late 1920s, when he also worked as a stand-in for Warner Baxter. After the war he began his association with John Ford, working in westerns such as *Fort Apache, 3 Godfathers, She Wore a Yellow Ribbon, Wagonmaster, Rio Grande,* and *The Searchers.* He also appeared in other westerns such as *Hondo, The Naked Spur, Pony Soldier, Apache War Smoke,* and *Westward the Women.*

In addition to stunt work, McGrath also appeared as an extra in many films throughout the 1940s and 1950s, and prior to *Wagon Train,* he worked in TV on *Cheyenne,* and *Tales of Wells Fargo.*

After his portrayal of Charlie Wooster on *Wagon Train,* he acted in TV series such as *Tammy, The Virginian, The Big Valley, and in the films Gunfight in Abilene, The War Wagon, Tammy and the Millionaire, The Reluctant Astronaut, The Last Challenge,* and *The Shakiest Gun in the West.*

JOHN MCINTIRE

John McIntire was raised in Montana and grew up amidst the western lifestyle, surrounded by cowboys and ranchers. After graduating from USC, he began his acting career in radio and on stage. His lengthy movie career began in 1947. He often played a variety of roles including policemen, doctors, military officers, professors, and clergymen. He also appeared in dozens of westerns and some of his best roles were in several Anthony Mann films such as *Winchester 73,* and *The Far Country.* In 1958, McIntire was cast as veteran detective Dan Muldoon in the 30-minute version of *The Naked City.* He later succeeded Ward Bond on *Wagon Train* (1961–1965), and Charles Bickford on *The Virginian* (1967–1970). His final film appearance was in *Turner and Hooch* in 1989.

His feature films include *Cloak and Dagger, Rooster Cogburn, Honky Tonk Man, Summer and Smoke, Two Rode Together, Flaming Star, Elmer Gantry, Psycho, The Tin Star, The Light in the Forest, Away All Boats, I've Lived Before, The Kentuckian, Stranger on Horseback, Apache, War Arrow, A Lion in the Streets, The President's Lady, The Mississippi Gambler, The Lawless Breed, Horizons West, The World in His Arms, Glory Alley, Westward the Women, The Raging Tide, The Tanks Are Coming, Under the Gun, Walk Softly Stranger, The Asphalt Jungle, No Sad Songs For Me, Down to the Sea in Ships, Ambush, Command Decision, The Street with No Name, Black Bart,* and *Call Northside 777.*

His television work includes *Dream Breakers, Aaron's Way, St. Elsewhere, The Love Boat, Different Strokes, Night Court, Trapper John M.D., The Yellow Rose, Hotel, Quincy M.E., The Incredible Hulk, Young Maverick, Shirley, Dallas, Fantasy Island, Charlie's Angels, Aspen, Longstreet, Love American Style, The F.B.I., Bonanza, A Man Called Shenandoah, The Fugitive, Daniel Boone, Arrest and Trial, Laramie, The Untouchables, The Twilight Zone, Alfred Hitchcock Presents, Peter Gunn, Zane Grey Theater, Wanted: Dead or Alive, Cimarron City* and *Father Knows Best.*

DENNY MILLER

After two years of military service in Germany, Denny Miller enrolled at UCLA as a student/athlete on a basketball scholarship, where he played (with younger brother Kent) for Hall of Fame Coach John Wooden, and earned a degree in physical education.

Miller was discovered by a Hollywood agent and subsequently placed under contract to M.G.M. He acted in several episodic TV shows, then appeared on screen in Vincent Minelli's *Some Came Running* in 1958, and starred in *Tarzan, the Ape Man* a year later.

The day after he graduated from UCLA, Miller signed a seven year contract with Revue Studios (which later became Universal). He appeared in television series such as *Overland Trail, Laramie, Riverboat, The Deputy, Wells Fargo, G.E. Theater,* and *Richard Diamond, Private Detective.* In 1961 he debuted as Duke Shannon in the latter part of *Wagon Train's* fourth year, and remained with the series for three more seasons. In the mid-60s, he co-starred with Juliet Prowse in the NBC series *Mona McCluskey.*

For the past four decades, Miller has appeared in numerous television shows, films and national commercials. He has also authored two books and won critical acclaim for his "modest, witty, self-deprecating humor, and skill for anecdotal raconteurism."

His film work includes *Hell to Pay, Circle of Power, Cabo Blanco, The Dion Brothers, The Norseman, The Island at the Top of the World, Buck and the Preacher, Armageddon, Making It, The Party,* and *Love in a Goldfish Bowl.*

His many television credits include: *Dr. Quinn, Medicine Woman, Lonesome Dove: The Series, Bordertown, Outlaws, Magnum P.I., Hardcastle and McCormick, Murder She Wrote, Matt Houston, The Fall Guy, Knight Rider, Hart to Hart, Dallas, Mickey Spillane's Mike Hammer, V, Simon and Simon, Buck Rogers in the 25th Century, The Incredible Hulk, Vegas, Charlie's Angels, MASH, Fantasy Island, Young Maverick, The Rockford Files, Battlestar Gallactica, Flying High, Barnaby Jones, Wonder Woman, Quincy M.E., Alice, Cannon, The Six Million Dollar Man, Mobile One, Emergency, The Streets of San Francisco, McCloud, Gunsmoke, Mission Impossible, The Virginian, Ironside, I Dream of Jeannie, Love American Style, The Name of the Game, Hawaii Five-O, The High Chaparral, Death Valley Days, I Spy, Gilligan's Island, The Fugitive, The Girl from Uncle, Run for Your Life, Ben Casey* and *The Rifleman.*

DEBRA PAGET

Blessed with beauty and talent, Debra Paget was placed under contract to Twentieth Century Fox at the age of 14. She co-starred in over 20 feature films throughout the 1950s, then began to guest star in a variety of network television shows. She retired from the acting profession in the mid-1960s, while still in her early 30s.

Her feature film work includes *Cry of the City, House of Strangers, Broken Arrow, Fourteen Hours, Bird of Paradise, Anne of the Indies, Belles on Their Toes, Les Miserables, Stars and Stripes Forever, Prince Valiant, Princess of the Nile, Demetrius and the Gladiators, The Gambler from Natchez, White Feather, Seven Angry Men, The Last Hunt, The Ten Commandments, Love Me Tender, The River's Edge, Omar Khayam, Journey to the Lost City, The Tiger of Eschnapur, The Indian Tomb, Cleopatra's Daughter, Why Must I Die?, Most Dangerous Man Alive, Rome 1585, Tales of Terror,* and *The Haunted Palace.*

Her television credits include *Burke's Law, Rawhide, Tales of Wells Fargo, The Millionaire, Johnny Ringo, The Dupont Show with June Allyson, The Man and the Challenge, Riverboat, Wagon Train, Cimarron City, Climax,* and *The 20th Century Fox Hour.*

GREG PALMER

Greg Palmer began his career as a radio announcer. In the 1950s he was signed to a contract at Universal International and appeared in a number of films there. From the 1950s through the early 1980s, Palmer appeared in numerous movies and television series, many of which were western, detective, and sci-fi adventures. A partial list of his films include *Early Warning, Scream, The Man with Bogart's Face, Hot Lead and Cold Feet, The Shootist, Big Jake, Rio Lobo, The McKenzie Break, Chisum, The Undefeated, Billion Dollar Brain, The Rare Breed, Shenandoah, The Quick Gun, Advance to the Rear, The Prize, 40 Pounds of Trouble, The Comancheros, The Cat Burglar, Most Dangerous Man Alive, The Absentminded Professor, Five Guns to Tombstone, The Shaggy Dog, Thundering Jets, From Hell It Came, Revolt at Fort Laramie, Hilda Crane, The Creature Walks Among Us, To Hell and Back, Magnificent Obsession, Playgirl, Taza, Son of Cochise, All American, The Veils of Baghdad, Column South,* and *It Happens Every Thursday.*

His television credits include: *The Blue and the Gray, Beggarman Thief, True Grit, Go West Young Girl, CHIPs, How the West Was Won, Quincy M.E., Disneyland, The New Daughters of Joshua Cabe, Gunsmoke, Kolchak: The Night Stalker, Alias Smith and Jones, Mongo's Back in Town, The Virginian, Menace on the Mountain, Death Valley Days, Bonanza, The Wild Wild West, Star Trek, Cimarron Strip, Mission Impossible, The High Chaparral, Tarzan, Gomer Pyle U.S.M.C., Laredo, Run Buddy Run, The Long Hot Summer, Get Smart, The Legend of Jesse James, Branded, The Big Valley, Run for Your Life, Rawhide, 77 Sunset Strip, Laramie, Have Gun Will Travel, Bronco, The Roaring 20s, Tales of Wells Fargo, The Life and Legend of Wyatt Earp, Outlaws, Cheyenne, The Tall Man, The Untouchables, Sugarfoot, Lawman, Wagon Train, Surfside 6, The Deputy, The Man from Blackhawk, Overland Trail, The Millionaire, Hotel de Paree, Shotgun Slade, Sea Hunt, The Restless Gun, Cimarron City, Buckskin, Frontier Doctor, The Texan, Broken Arrow, Sky King, Sergeant Preston of the Yukon, The Public Defender,* and *Highway Patrol.*

NEHEMIAH PERSOFF

After training at the Actors Studio with Elia Kazan and later with Lee Strasberg, Nehemiah Persoff made his Broadway debut in *Galileo*. Throughout the 1950s he appeared in numerous Broadway plays, in many live television shows, and in feature films. In 1960 he joined the group of New York actors who moved to California. Persoff continued to act in features and appeared frequently in episodic television, TV movies and mini-series over the next three decades. He retired from acting in the early 1990s to concentrate on painting.

Film credits include: *The Last Temptation of Christ, Twins, Yentil, Voyage of the Damned, The People Next Door, Red Sky at Morning, Mrs. Pollifax Spy, The Girl Who Knew Too Much, Mafia, Panic in the Streets, The Money Jungle, The Power, Too Many Thieves, The Greatest Story Ever Told, The Global Affair, Fate Is the Hunter, The Hook, The Comancheros, The Big Show, Never Steal Anything Small, Green Mansions, Al Capone, Some Like It Hot, Day of the Outlaw, The Badlanders, Street of Sinners, Men in War, This Angry Age, The Wrong Man, The Harder They Fall,* and *On the Waterfront*.

His many television appearances include: *Reasonable Doubts, Murder She Wrote, Star Trek: The Next Generation, Law and Order, Hunter, Highway to Heaven, Magnum P.I., L.A. Law, MacGiver, Hotel, Fantasy Island, Barney Miller, Vegas, Quincy M.E., The Hardy Boys, The Invisible Man, Police Woman, Baretta, Police Story, Cannon, The Bionic Woman, The Six Million Dollar Man, Love American Style, Mannix, McCloud, Marcus Welby M.D., The Streets of San Francisco, Dan August, Hawaii Five-0, The Mod Squad, Gunsmoke, High Chaparral, The Name of the Game, Mission Impossible, Gilligan's Island, The Flying Nun, The Time Tunnel, The Big Valley, A Man Called Shenandoah, The Man from Uncle, The Wild Wild West, The Legend of Jesse James, Honey West, I Spy, Mr. Novak, Burke's Law, Ben Casey, Rawhide, The Trials of O'Brien, The Dick Powell Theater, Thriller, Voyage to the Bottom of the Sea, The Untouchables, Route 66, Naked City, Alfred Hitchcock Presents, Wagon Train, Twilight Zone,* and *Playhouse 90*.

JOSEPH PEVNEY

Joseph Pevney began his career as an actor on the New York stage. He subsequently began to appear in films in the late 1940s such as *Nocturne, Body and Soul, The Street with No Name, Thieves Highway, Outside the Wall*, and *Shakedown.*

He began his directorial career in 1950 and made over thirty feature films mainly for Universal International, and several at Warner Bros. through 1961. From the early 1960s through the mid-1980s, he directed several hundred episodic television shows.

His many network television credits include: *Trapper John M.D., A Family Affair, Little House on the Prairie, Palmertown U.S.A., Hager, The Rockford Files, Mysterious Island of Beautiful Women (MOW), How the West Was Won, The Incredible Hulk, Executive Suite, Sword of Justice, The Paper Chase, Fantasy Island, The Hardy Boys, Emergency, Mobile One, Who Is the Black Dahlia (MOW), Petrocelli, My Darling Daughters' Anniversary (MOW), Search, Bonanza, The Partners, Cades County, The High Chaparral, The Virginian, Marcus Welby, Adam 12, Star Trek, Mission Impossible, Laredo, T.H.E. Cat, The Fugitive, Twelve O'Clock High, Pistols 'n' Petticoats, The Legend of Jesse James, The Munsters, The Loner, The Big Valley, Kraft Suspense Theater, The Alfred Hitchcock Hour, Bewitched, Wagon Train, Going My Way, Ben Casey, The New Breed*, and *Bus Stop.*

His feature films include *Night of the Grizzly, Portrait of a Mobster, The Plunderers, The Crowded Sky, Cash McCall, Torpedo Run, Twilight for the Gods, Man of a Thousand Faces, The Midnight Story, Tammy and the Bachelor, Istanbul, Away All Boats, Congo Crossing, Female on the Beach, Foxfire, Six Bridges to Cross, 3-Ring Circus, Playgirl, Yankee Pasha, Back to God's Country, It Happens Every Thursday, Desert Legion, Because of You, Just Across the Street, Flesh and Fury, Meet Danny Wilson, The Strange Door, The Lady from Texas, Iron Man, Air Cadet, Undercover Girl*, and *Shakedown.*

SLIM PICKENS

Slim Pickens began his life as a real cowboy on the rodeo circuit while a teenager. He later began a 20-year career as a rodeo clown, appearing throughout the country.

In the early 1950s, Pickens began to appear in western films and played a variety of comic and villainous roles in movies and television over the next thirty years. His extensive film work includes *Honeysuckle Rose, Tom Horn, The Black Hole, 1941, Beyond the Poseidon Adventure, The Swarm, White Line Fever, The Apple Dumpling Gang, Pat Garrett and Billy the Kid, The Getaway, The Honkers, The Ballad of Cable Hogue, Will Penny, Rough Night in Jericho, In Harm's Way, Major Dundee,* and *Doctor Strangelove or How I Learned to Stop Worrying and Love the Bomb.*

His many network television credits include *Filthy Rich, The Nashville Palace, B.J. and the Bear, The Love Boat, The Misadventures of Sheriff Lobo, The Sacketts, How the West Was Won, The Life and Times of Grizzly Adams, Baretta, McMillan and Wife, Disneyland, Kung Fu, Hawaii Five-O, Night Gallery, The Partridge Family, Alias Smith and Jones, Gunsmoke, Medical Center, That Girl, Ironside, Mannix, Custer, Run for Your Life, Daniel Boone, The Legend of Jesse James, Rawhide, The Fugitive, The Man from Uncle, The Alfred Hitchcock Hour, Wagon Train, The Tall Man, Outlaws, The Westerner, Surfside Six, Riverboat, Sugarfoot, Route 66, Maverick, Overland Trail, Cheyenne, Lassie,* and *Annie Oakley.*

TOMMY SANDS

Tommy Sands began performing country music at the tender age of 8 at a Shreveport, LA radio station. In 1951, he recorded his first tune for Freedom Records, and a year later he signed with RCA records where he recorded for three years. In 1957, Sands guest-starred on an episode of *Kraft Television Theatre* entitled *The Singing Idol.* He performed the song *"Teenage Crush"* which became a charted hit and rose to Number 3 on the pop charts. In 1958, he starred in the film *Sing Boy Sing* which was said to have been a biography of his career. Over the next twenty years, Sands appeared in films and guested on network TV.

His film resume includes *Mardi Gras, Love in a Goldfish Bowl, Babes in Toyland, The Longest Day, Ensign Pulver, None But the Brave,* and *The Violent Ones. His TV appearances include The Hardy Boys/Nancy Drew Mysteries, Hawaii Five-O, Bonanza, Branded, Mr. Novak, Combat, Kraft Suspense Theater, Slattery's People, Wagon Train, Laramie, Alcoa Premiere, The United States Steel Hour, Frontier Justice, Studio One, Shower of Stars,* and *Zane Gray Theater.*

PAUL SAVAGE

Paul Savage was an Executive Story Consultant on the television series *Gunsmoke* (in addition to writing numerous episodes). He became one of the top western television writers in the episodic genre, and enjoyed a prolific career. He also wrote the story for the feature film *Inchon* (starring Sir Laurence Olivier) and the screenplay for the Disney film *The Wild Country*.

His writing credits include: *Murder She Wrote, Bonanza: The Next Generation, Matlock, MacGyver, Air Wolf, Jessie, The Yellow Rose, The Mississippi, Walking Tall, Marciano (MOW), The Dukes of Hazzard, The Waltons, Gibbsville, The Quest, The New Daughters of Joshua Cabe (MOW), Mackintosh and T.J., Barbary Coast, The Rookies, The Girls at Huntington House (MOW), The Daughters of Joshua Cabe (MOW), Cutter's Trail (MOW), The Big Valley, A Man Called Shenandoah, Daniel Boone, Temple Houston, 77 Sunset Strip, Laramie, Kraft Mystery Theater, Lawman, Ben Casey, King of Diamonds, Surfside Six, Klondike, Westinghouse Desilu Playhouse, Mackenzie's Raiders, This Man Dawson, The Rough Riders, Whispering Smith, Wagon Train, Tombstone Territory,* and *Casey Jones.*

WILLIAM SMITH

William Smith, a direct descendant of Daniel Boone and Kit Carson, has a touch of Pioneer in his blood. Born on his Dad's cattle ranch in Columbia, Missouri, he was riding horses before he could walk. After losing everything to the Depression and the Dustbowl, the Smith family moved to California. Bill became a studio extra, appearing in hundreds of films as a child performer. After high school, Bill joined the Air Force. Being fluent in five languages: English, Russian, German, French, and Serbo-Croatian, he was assigned overseas to the NSA and the CIA, active in military intelligence during the Korean War.

After receiving a Purple Heart for his military duty, Smith studied at the Sorbonne in Paris, the University of Munich, and Syracuse University. Graduating cum laude at UCLA, he received a Master's in Russian Area Studies. With only forty hours remaining to complete his doctorate, he dropped out of academia and was put under contract by MGM.

Smith soon gained recognition, becoming one of Hollywood's best-known character actors, appearing in over two hundred movies, and hundreds of television episodes. He became a regular in such TV series as *Asphalt Jungle, Laredo, Zero One, Hawaii Five-O, and Wildside.* His western TV guest appearances include *Gunsmoke, Daniel Boone, Wagon Train, Guns of Will Sonnett, Alias Smith & Jones, The Virginian, Death Valley Days, Kung Fu, The Oregon Trail, Guns of Paradise, Here Come the Brides, Stoney Burke, Custer, Bearcats, Seven Brides for Seven Brothers, The Yellow Rose, The Young Riders,* and *Walker, Texas Ranger.*

In spite of his scholarly background, his dangerous good looks made him a natural to be cast in the black hat. Some of these more notable performances are as the outlaw in *The Ultimate Warrior,* as Gene Wilder's nemesis in *The Frisco Kid,* and the Russian Colonel in John Milius' *Red Dawn.* He took screen villainy to new heights as Falconetti in the television series *Rich Man, Poor Man.*

Now and then Bill does get to play a good guy, as with Kurt Russell in *Mean Season,* as Schwarzenegger's awesome father in *Conan the Barbarian,* and the fighter set up to do battle with Clint Eastwood in *Any Which Way You Can.* Bill, a two-time World Arm Wrestling Champion and sports record holder, continues his acting career and has become an avid poet of note.

WARREN STEVENS

Warren Stevens trained at the Neighborhood Playhouse in New York. After serving as a pilot in the U.S. Air Force during world War II, he began working in radio and performing in summer stock. In the late 1940s he joined the Actor's Studio where he worked with Elia Kazan.

He was later cast in *Detective Story* on Broadway which led to a contract at 20th Century Fox in the 1950s. He made his movie debut in *Follow the Sun,* and throughout the next two decades he appeared in such films as *The Frogman, Phone Call from a Stranger, Deadline U.S.A., O'Henry's Full House, The Barefoot Contessa, Black Tuesday, Forbidden Planet, The Price of Fear, On the Threshold of Space, Hot Spell, The Case Against Brooklyn, Intent to Kill, No Name on the Bullet, 40 Pounds of Trouble, Madame X, An American Dream,* and *Madigan.*

Over a period of five decades, he guest-starred in hundreds of network television shows such as *E.R., The Twilight Zone, Falcon Crest,*

Quincy M.E., The Rebels, Wonder Woman, Police Woman, MASH, Petrocelli, Marcus Welby, Cannon, Ironside, Mission Impossible, Adam-12, The Virginian, Mod Squad, Bonanza, The Name of the Game, Land of the Giants, Mannix, Star Trek, The Iron Horse, Voyage to the Bottom of the Sea, The High Chaparral, T.H.E. Cat, Tarzan, Daniel Boone, The Rat Patrol, The Time Tunnel, Combat, Bob Hope Presents the Chrysler Theater, The Man from Uncle, I Spy, Rawhide, Honey West, Profiles in Courage, The Outer Limits, The Richard Boone Show, Have Gun-Will Travel, Gunsmoke, Route 66, Hawaiian Eye, Wagon Train, Surfside Six, Checkmate, The Defenders, The Untouchables, Adventures in Paradise, Hong Kong, Mr. Lucky, Laramie, and *One Step Beyond.*

BUCK TAYLOR

Born the son of well-known character actor Dub Taylor, Buck Taylor initially took a different path, studying art at the University of Southern California and trying out for the U.S. Olympic Gymnastics team. But the acting profession came calling. He began to appear in a wide variety of television shows from *The Adventures of Ozzie and Harriet* and *My Favorite Martian,* to the classic period westerns such as *Have Gun Will Travel* and *The Rebel.* Taylor is best remembered for his portrayal of Newly O'Brien on *Gunsmoke* (1967–1975). In addition to becoming an accomplished western artist specializing in watercolors, Taylor has also been honored by various prestigious western associations.

His film work includes *The Mist, The Wendell Baker Story, Wild Michigan, The Hard Ride, Miracle at Sage Creek, Hell to Pay, Truce, The Alamo, Gods and Generals, Jericho, Comanche, Wild Wild West, Tombstone, Gettysburg, Big Bad John, Payback,* and *Triumphs of a Man Called Horse.*

His many television credits include: *Comanche Moon, The Soul Collector, Hard Time, Rough Riders, Dallas: JR Returns, Conagher, Proud Men, Gunsmoke: Return to Dodge, Timestalkers, Down the Long Hills, Dream West, All American Cowboy, Wild Horse, No Man's Land, Wild Times, The Sacketts, The Busters, Standing Tall, Walker, Texas Ranger, The Young Riders, Dallas, Knots Landing, Paradise, T.J. Hooker, Matt Houston, The Fall Guy, Daniel Boone, Wagon Train, The Virginian, The Big Valley, Bonanza, Alfred Hitchcock Presents, Ben Casey, The Fugitive, The Outer Limits,* and *Stoney Burke.*

GREGORY WALCOTT

Gregory Walcott grew up in a small eastern North Carolina town before hitchhiking his way to Hollywood in 1949. Over the next 40 years, he became one of the better character actors in the business, appearing in over 50 movies and 300 television shows. He was featured in such memorable films as *Mr. Roberts* and *Battle Cry*, and praised by critics for his co-starring role with Tony Curtis in *The Outsider*, the epic Marine film about the flag raising on Iwo Jima.

His feature film credits include *Ed Wood, House 11-The Second Story, Tilt, Norma Rae, Every Which Way But Loose, Midway, The Eiger Sanction, Thunderbolt and Lightfoot, The Last American Hero, Joe Kidd, Prime Cut, Bill Wallace of China* (also produced), *Captain Newman M.D., Badman's Country, Jet Attack, The Persuader, Thunder Over Arizona, The Steel Jungle, The Lieutenant Wore Skirts, The Court Martial of Billy Mitchell, Texas Lady, The McConnell Story,* and *Strange Lady in Town.*

His many television appearances include *Murder She Wrote, Dallas, Simon and Simon, Air Wolf, Alice, Dynasty, The Dukes of Hazzard, The Contender, CHIPs, Baretta, Sharks, Barnaby Jones, The Six Million Dollar Man, Eight Is Enough, McCloud, The Quest, Gemini Man, Kojak, The Invisible Man, Little House on the Prairie, Police Story, Chase, Bonanza, The Mod Squad, The High Chaparral, Daniel Boone, The Big Valley, Shane, A Man Called Shenandoah, Rawhide, G.E. True, The Dakotas, Laramie, 87th Precinct* (series regular), *The Deputy, Tales of Wells Fargo, Bat Masterson, Wagon Train, Riverboat, The Life and Legend of Wyatt Earp, The Tall Man, Tombstone Territory, Dennis the Menace, The Rifleman, Maverick, Trackdown, Perry Mason, Sugarfoot, Zane Grey Theater, Navy Log, Cheyenne,* and *Cavalcade of America.*

BEVERLY WASHBURN

In the 1950s Beverly Washburn became one of the busiest child actors in movies and television, and continued her career into adulthood. Her films credits include *Summer Love, Old Yeller, The Lone Ranger, The Juggler, Shane, Hans Christian Andersen, The Greatest Show on Earth, Superman and the Mole-Men, Here Comes the Groom,* and *The Killer That Stalked New York.*

Her many television credits include: *Las Vegas, Children of the Dark, Scarecrow and Mrs. King, Disneyland, The Streets of San Francisco, Most Wanted, The Manhunter, Getting Together, Star Trek, Gidget, The Patty Duke Show, Mr. Novak, Arrest and Trial, 77 Sunset Strip, Wagon Train, Hawaiian Eye, The New Loretta Young Show, Target: The Corruptors, Thriller, The Law and Mrs. Jones, The Texan, Leave It to Beaver, One Step Beyond, General Electric Theater, Jane Wyman Presents The Fireside Theatre, Schlitz Playhouse of Stars, Zane Gray Theater, Four Start Playhouse, Fury, Science Fiction Theater, Fireside Theatre, Dragnet, Lux Video Theatre,* and *The Jack Benny Program.*

TERRY WILSON

Terry Wilson originally planned to be a veterinarian attending California Polytechnic School on a football scholarship. He enlisted in the marines during World War II then began doing stunts after the war through a friend at Warner Bros. Wilson worked on a lot of John Ford films with Frank McGrath whom he had met years before on a film at MGM. Originally Wilson was hired as a stunt man and double for Ward Bond on *Wagon Train*, but as the series progressed he developed as an actor and became the assistant wagonmaster.

After the show ended, Wilson worked on other series and in 1977 he was production supervisor for *The Oregon Trail*, a series filmed at Universal. He later became V.P. of a construction firm in Southern California.

His film and television credits include *The Dukes of Hazzard, The Treasure Seekers, Escape to Witch Mountain, The Daughters of Joshua Cabe Return, Hitchhike, Banacek, Westworld, One Little Indian, Rage, Gunsmoke, Fair Play, Support Your Local Gunfighter, The Virginian, Dirty Dingus Magee, The Savage Land, The Shakiest Gun in the West, A Man Called Gannon, Hondo, The War Wagon, The Plainsman, The Wings of Eagles, Pillar of the Sky, Tension at Table Rock, The Last Hunt, The Searchers, The Last Frontier, Seven Brides for Seven Brothers,* and *Westward the Women.*

MORGAN WOODWARD

After enlisting in the U.S. Army Air Corps Pilot Training Program and serving in World War II, Morgan Woodward began his professional acting career with the renowned Margo Jones Repertory Theatre in Dallas. Later, while attending the University of Texas, Woodward had his own radio show, a dance band, as well as a barbershop quartet.

After graduating with a BBA degree, Woodward entered the University of Texas Law School, but his studies were interrupted when he was recalled to active duty with the Air Force and sent to Korea with the Military Air Transport Command.

Following the war, Woodward came to the attention of Walt Disney who cast him in *The Great Locomotive Chase*, Disney's first full-length feature film. Impressed, Disney signed Woodward for two more films. Shortly after, Woodward signed a four-year contract to star with Hugh O'Brian on the top-rated television series *Wyatt Earp*.

Over the next four decades Woodward appeared in over 250 TV and motion picture films. He holds the record for having done more guest starring roles on the TV series *Gunsmoke* (19) and appearances on *Wagon Train* (12) than any other actor. He starred in the MGM TV series *Logan's Run* (1977–1978) and also in the top-rated daytime series *Days of Our Lives* (1987–1988). Woodward was also a regular guest star on *Dallas* for several years where he portrayed the character Punk Anderson.

In 1988, Woodward was given the Golden Lariat Award at the National Western Film Festival. In August of that same year he received the prestigious Golden Boot Award from the Hollywood Motion Picture and Television Fund. In 1994, the Texas Arts Council presented Woodward with its Lifetime Achievement in the Arts Award in his hometown of Arlington, Texas. The City also named a prominent street "Morgan Woodward Way" in August of 1995. Woodward has also restored and rebuilt antique airplanes, and is recognized in aviation circles as an authority on early American aircraft.

His many network TV credits include *Millennium, The X Files, Matlock, 21 Jump Street, The A-Team, T.J. Hooker, Dukes of Hazzard, Knight Rider, Scarecrow and Mrs. King, Hill Street Blues, CHiPs, Centennial, How the West Was Won, Deadly Game, The Quest, The Longest Drive, The Last Day, The Hatfields and The McCoys, The Waltons, Kung Fu, McMillan and Wife, Cannon, Bonanza, Yuma, It Takes a Thief, Star Trek, The High Chaparral, The Big Valley, Daniel Boone, Temple Houston, The Virginian, Have Gun-Will Travel, The Restless Gun*, and *Zane Gray Theater*.

Feature film work includes *Battle Beyond the Stars, Speed Trap, Final Chapter-Walking Tall, Which Way Is Up?, The Killing of a Chinese Bookie, The Midnight Man, One Little Indian, Running Wild, Death of a*

Gunfighter, Westward Ho the Wagons!, Firecreek, Cool Hand Luke, Gunpoint, and *Ride a Crooked Trail.*

DANA WYNTER

Dana Wynter has led an interesting life as an actress, author, journalist and activist. She began her life in Berlin and later spent her formative years in Scotland and England. After a year of medical study at Rhodes University in South Africa, she returned to England and began to work in the English theater. In the early 1950s she went to New York and subsequently appeared in live television and on Broadway. After being offered contracts by three Hollywood studios, Wynter signed a seven-year deal with 20th Century Fox in 1955. She starred in a number of feature films on into the early 1960s, then began to guest star in numerous network TV series.

In the mid-1960s, Wynter took up journalism with her own by-line in *The Guardian* (the oldest and most prestigious English newspaper). She also wrote articles for *National Review, Country Living, Image, The Irish Times*, and others. In recent years her book *Other People, Other Places*, (essays about her life and memories on four continents) was published by Caladrius Press, Dublin.

Her film work includes *View from Pompey's Head, D-Day—Sixth of June, Invasion of the Body Snatchers, Something of Value, Fraulein, In Love and War, Shake Hands with the Devil, Sink the Bismarck, On the Double, The List of Adrian Messinger, Airport*, and Santee.

Her many television appearances include *Dana Wynter in Ireland (PBS), The Royal Romance of Charles and Diana (MOW), Backstairs at the White House (mini series), Magnum P.I., Hart to Hart, The Love Boat, Hawaii Five-O, Fantasy Island, City of Angels, Ellery Queen, Medical Center, Cannon, Ironside, Owen Marshall—Counselor at Law, Marcus Welby, Gunsmoke, Love American Style, The Name of the Game, The Invaders, The Wild Wild West, The Man Who Never Was, The F.B.I., Twelve O'Clock High, The Rogues, The Alfred Hitchcock Hour, Wagon Train, The Virginian, The Dick Powell Theater, Playhouse 90, Twentieth Century Fox Hour, Studio One, U.S. Steel Hour*, and *Suspicion.*

RECOMMENDED READING

Alias Smith and Jones. Sandra K. Sagala and Joanne M. Bragwell, Bearmanor Media.

Best of the Badmen. Boyd Magers, Empire Publishers.

The Cisco Kid: American Hero, Hispanic Roots. Francis Nevins, Bilingual Press/Arizona State University.

Cowboy Corner Conversations. Red Steagall, State House Press.

Didn't You Used to Be What's His Name? Denny Miller, To Health With You Publishers.

The Films of Audie Murphy. Bob Larkins and Boyd Magers, McFarland & Company.

Gene Autry Westerns. Boyd Magers, Empire Publishers.

Gunsmoke—An American Institution: Celebrating 50 Years of Television's Best Western. Ben Costello, Five Star Publications.

Have Gun Will Travel. Martin Grams and Les Rayburn, OTR Publishers.

A History of Television's The Virginian 1962–1971. Paul Green, McFarland & Company.

Hopalong Cassidy: On the Page, On the Screen. Francis Nevins, Lone Pine Film Museum.

Ladies of the Western. Boyd Magers and Michael Fitzgerald, McFarland & Company.

The Official TV Western Round-Up Book. Neil Summers and Roger M. Crowley, Old West Publishing.

A Reference Guide to Television's Bonanza. Bruce Leiby and Linda Leiby, McFarland & Company.

So You Wanna See Cowboy Stuff (The Western Movie/TV Tour Guide). Boyd Magers, Empire Publishers.

John Wayne: An American Legend. Roger M. Crowley, Old West Publishing

Western's Women. Boyd Magers and Michael Fitzgerald, McFarland & Company

Guy Williams: The Man Behind the Mask. Antoinette Girgenti Lane, Bearmanor Media.

The Zorro TV Companion. Gerry Dooley, McFarland & Company.

END NOTES
Telephone Interviews by Author

1. Harry Carey, Jr., January 2008, California.
2. Gary Yoggy (from his book: *Riding the Video Range: The Rise and Fall of the Western on Television*, McFarland and Company, 2008).
3. Robert Horton, February 2008, California.
4. Boyd Magers, January 2008, New Mexico.
5. L. Q. Jones, February 2008, California.
6. Greg Palmer, January 2008, California.
7. Gregory Walcott, January 2008, California.
8. Beverly Washburn, February 2008, Nevada.
9. Debra Paget, January 2008, Texas.
10. James H. Brown, February 2008, California.
11. Denny Miller (from his book *Didn't You Used to Be What's His Name?* To Health With You Publishers, 2004.)
12. Ernest Borgnine, January 2008, California.
13. James Drury, March 2008, Texas.
14. Paul Savage, January 2008, California.
15. Dana Wynter, January 2008, California.
16. John Christie, January 2008, California.
17. Frederick Shorr, January 2008, California.
18. James Lydon, January 2008, California.
19. Joseph Pevney, January 2008, California.
20. Denny Miller, January and February 2008, Nevada.

21. Robert Horton (From the *Western Clippings* Interview, 1999).
22. Robert Horton (from the *TV Guide* Interview, June 1961).
23. Morgan Woodward, February 2008, California.
24. Robert Fuller, February 2008, Texas.
25. Harry Flynn, January 2008, California.
26. Tommy Sands, January 2008, California.
27. Peter Brown, March 2008, Arizona.
28. Warren Stevens, February 2008, California.
29. Diane Foster, January 2008, California.

ABOUT THE
AUTHOR

BORN AND RAISED in Philadelphia, James Rosin graduated from Temple University's School of Communications with a degree in broadcasting. In New York, he studied acting with Bobby Lewis and appeared in plays off-off Broadway and on the ABC soap opera, *Edge of Night*. In Los Angeles, Rosin played featured and costarring roles in such TV series as Mickey Spillane's *Mike Hammer, T. J. Hooker, Quincy M.E., The Powers of Matthew Star, Cannon, Mannix, Banacek, Adam-12, Love, American Style*, and two miniseries, *Loose Change* and *Once an Eagle*. His film credits include *Up Close and Personal, Sleepers* and *The Adventures of Buckaroo Banzai*. He also wrote stories and teleplays for *Quincy M.E.* (NBC), *Capitol* (CBS), and *Loving Friends and Perfect Couples* (Showtime). His full-length play, *Michael in Beverly Hills*, a comedy-drama, premiered at American Theater Arts in Los Angeles and was later presented off-off Broadway, at the American Musical Dramatic Academy's Studio One Theater.

In recent years, Rosin has written and produced two one-hour sports documentaries, which have aired on public television: *Philly Hoops: The SPHAS and Warriors* (about the first two professional basketball teams in Philadelphia) and *The Philadelphia Athletics 1901–1954* (about the former American League franchise). His first book, *Philly Hoops: The SPHAS and Warriors*, was published in October of 2003, followed by *Rock, Rhythm & Blues*, in 2004, *Philadelphia: City of Music*, (2006), *Route 66: The Television Series 1960–1964*, (2007), and *Naked City: The Television Series,* (2008). He has also been a contributing writer to *Classic Images* and *Films of the Golden Age Magazine*.